Be the HU

Also by Harold Klemp

The Book of ECK Parables, Volume 1
The Book of ECK Parables, Volume 2
The Book of ECK Parables, Volume 3
Child in the Wilderness
The Living Word
Riding for the ECK Brand
Soul Travelers of the Far Country
The Wind of Change
Wisdom of the Heart

The Mahanta Transcripts Series

Journey of Soul, Book 1
How to Find God, Book 2
The Secret Teachings, Book 3
The Golden Heart, Book 4
Cloak of Consciousness, Book 5
Unlocking the Puzzle Box, Book 6
The Eternal Dreamer, Book 7

This book has been authored by and published under the supervision of the Living ECK Master, Sri Harold Klemp. It is the Word of ECK.

Be the HU

Harold Klemp

ECKANKAR
Minneapolis, MN

Be the HU

Copyright © 1992 ECKANKAR

All rights reserved. No part of this book may be reproduced, stored in a retrieval system, or transmitted in any form by any means, whether electronic, mechanical, photocopying, recording, or otherwise without written permission of ECKANKAR.

The terms ECKANKAR, ECK, EK, MAHANTA, SOUL TRAVEL, and VAIRAGI, among others, are trademarks of ECKANKAR, P.O. Box 27300, Minneapolis, MN 55427 U.S.A.

Printed in U.S.A.
Library of Congress Catalog Card Number: 92-72946

Compiled from the talks of Sri Harold Klemp by Mary Carroll Moore
Edited by Joan Klemp
Anthony Moore

Cover design by Lois Stanfield
Illustrations by Fraser MacDonald

If you make yourself more and more one with the HU, you will find that life is a more joyful place.

Contents

Introduction xiii

Part One: Awakening to Spirit

1. **The Purpose of Soul Travel** 3
   Converting the God Stuff • Living in This World • Strong in ECK • Self-Surrender • What about the Mind? • When We Remember Dreams—and When We Don't • Purification Process • How to Contemplate • Can Soul Ever Fall? • Soul-Mate Fallacy • A Marriage of Souls

2. **Path to Self-Mastery** 13
   Looking for a Master • States of Consciousness • The Living ECK Master and the Mahanta • As We Grow Spiritually • Working with the Spiritual Exercises • Benefits of HU • What Are Dreams, Really? • Darshan

3. **Taking Action** 21
   Meeting ECK Masters • What Can and Cannot Limit You • Who Else Studies ECK? • Important to Take Action • Facing Karma • Everything Depends on You • Types of Healing • Bringing Back Inner Experiences • A Little Boost

4. **Clear Vehicles for Divine Spirit** 31
   How We Get Used by ECK • Lightening the Load of Fear • Let the Light Shine • Assurance of the Presence of Spirit • What We Learn from Illness • Why Surrender? • More Than Just a Good Idea • Forming a Satsang Class • Go Slowly, Spiritually • Other Ways of Fasting • Am I Making Progress in ECK? • A Gentle Technique

5. When the Chela Is Ready 43
   Working with New Systems • Careful Planning • Rest Periods in ECK • Getting Spiritual Training • The True Realization • When the Chela Is Ready • How God Speaks to Us

6. Service to Something Greater 51
   Giving Out What You Receive • The Fire Within • The Spirit of the Law • Breaking Free • Rewinning Heaven Every Day • First Touch of God-Realization • Waking Yourself Up • False Problems • What Lies Ahead • Perfect Guidance • Degrees of Love • Exercising Your Spiritual Option

7. Spiritual Co-workers 61
   ECK Outreach • Helping Others Across • Is Your Religion Helping You? • Silent Witnesses • Try to Serve People • ECK and Drugs Don't Mix • New Forms of Healing • Kind Words before Translation • Letting Others Learn • Handling Future Changes • That Was Smooth!

8. Riding the Waves of Change 71
   When Positive and Negative Meet • Finding Out Who Loves Truth • A Practical Life in ECK • Hearing the Hidden Message • When Waves of Change Come • Aspects of Being a Co-worker • Cycles in the Lower Worlds

9. Responsibility and Spiritual Freedom 81
   When You Challenge What You Hear • How to Approach Your Lessons • Where Personal Freedom Stops • Becoming Spiritual Adults • Building for the Long Term

10. A Leap in Consciousness 87
    Frozen in Time • Keeping Up with ECK • Responsibility toward Self • Being Spiritually Fluid • Gaining Confidence, Losing Fear • Good Guidance • Is It Really ECK? • Why People Have Problems

Part Two: Following Your Dream

11. Following Your Dream 97
    The Mapmaker • Finding Our New Home • Rugged Makes Hardy

12. The Mission of Soul 103
    Coloring Pictures • Moving to a New Level • Spiritual Eyesight • What Is the Blue Star? • Keeping ECKANKAR Current • Leave the Past in the Past • A Spiritual Pace for Learning • Meeting Other Masters • When Soul Chooses to Leave

13. Year of Spiritual Healing 111
    Healing as You Evolve • Trying Something New • Practice Discrimination • Finishing Cycles You Begin • Sacredness of Initiate Reports

14. Your Freedom of Choice 117
    How We Learn to Make Choices • The Best-Laid Plans • Using the Creative Insight of Soul • Advice Is a Funny Thing • Practicing the Spiritual Exercises • When Love Is Missing • Nurturing What We Love

15. For the ECK Arahata 125
    Teaching Techniques • Procrastination Hides Fear • From Dry Doctrine to Stories • Encountering Inner Tests • Difference between Light and Sound

16. A New Level of Awareness 131
    The Voids between Planes • Moving Past Comfort Zones • How the Laws Reverse • Fasting in Times of Trouble • Out of the Void

17. The Law of Gratitude 137
    "What Exactly Is ECK?" • Awareness of Life • Gifts of Grace • An Understanding of Mind Scans • Keeping Clear • Long-Term Effects of Mind Scans • Law of Silence

18. The Evolving Shariyat 145
    Firsthand Experience • The Inner Side of Writing • Change Is a Natural Process • It's Not in a Book • Putting Your Heart into Life • Deadlines • Illustrating Truth

19. Opening the Loving Heart 151
    Recognizing Unfoldment • Spiritual Warmth • From the Higher Planes • Cleansing the Soul Body • When Consciousness Fades • Be Concerned with Your Life, Not Others

20. Spiritual Healings.. 159
    Spiritual Heart of ECK • ECK Healers • A Different
    Kind of Weather Report • What Caused It? • Accept the
    Physical • Chased by Spirits • Talk, but Mostly Listen

Part Three: Becoming a Co-worker

21. A True Missionary for ECK........................ 169
    Unexpected Gifts • A Different Kind of Missionary •
    One Step Further • Turkey Potpie • "There's Something Special about You" • In a Quiet Way

22. The Curtain between Cause and Effect.... 177
    Priests in ECK • The Issue of Abortion • Milarepa's
    Stone House • Respect for Others • How Initiate
    Reports Work Off Karma • Back Down the Mountain
    • What Is True Revelation?

23. Soul Equals Soul 187
    Learning to Work Together • A Historical Moment •
    Giving Up What You Outgrow • Soul Equals Soul •
    Moving ECKANKAR to the Next Step • The Temple
    of ECK • Are You Part of Life?

24. Your Life as Holy Ground 195
    Are You an ECKist Too? • Sacred Routines • Resistance to Change • A Broader Perspective: The Goal of
    ECK • Moving to the Causal Initiation • Holy Ground

25. Expressions of Divine Love 203
    Less Time but More Love • Feeding Insight • The
    Common Bond of Love • A New Haircut • Natural
    Balance • Shortages • Letting Divine Spirit Work in
    Your Life

26. Partners with Life 209
    False Jumps • Spiritual Growth Is a Process • Unity
    of Consciousness • Kind to Ourselves • Agree to
    Disagree • Careful Changes • Why Resistance Is a
    Blessing

27. Giving to ECKANKAR 217
    Vahana Teams • What We Offer the Seeker • Four
    Celebrations of Life • Youth Vahanas • What Is
    Burnout? • Needs of the Heart

28. **You Are Always Learning** 225
    Recording Stories • Learning about Yourself • Learning about Others • When ECK Taps You on the Shoulder • Learning about Excellence

29. **Fabric of God Consciousness** 233
    A Rite of Passage • Right Way and Wrong Way • Passing the Blame • When Your Idols Have Clay Feet • First Stage of Co-workership

30. **The Community of ECK** 241
    Forming the ECK Community • What Brand Are You Riding For? • What Is Not ECK • Coping with Change • The Umbrella of Your Culture • One of a Kind • How to Be There for Others • Areas of Service for High Initiates • Words and Actions

31. **Riding for the ECK Brand** 251
    Gifts of Energy • Living on the Edge • Cultivating Out the Weeds in ECK • A Mouse Nest • Problems Prevent Boredom • Why We Must Take Risks • Where ECK Meets the World • ECK Teamwork • Take a Chance in ECK • The Importance of Listening • A Love for All Life • Overcoming Prejudices • Are You an Open Doorway or a Locked Gate?

32. **Love Is All There Is** 263
    Take a Good Look • Developing Our Community • Are You Being Served? • Resolving Your Differences with Others • The ECK Temple in History • Being with Others in ECK • When You Hear the Sound • Life Always Expands

33. **Be the HU** 271
    Serving with Love • Truth Is More Than Talk • Who Is Guiding You? • Sharing Knowledge • Look behind the Lessons • Your Fear Bumper • Personal Battlegrounds • Living Life with Joy • Be a Spiritual Exercise • Your True Identity

Glossary 281

Bibliography 283

Sri Harold Klemp addresses those attending an ECK Worship Service at the Temple of ECK in Chanhassen, Minnesota. His straight-to-the-heart talks are a great gift. They pull aside the curtain of illusion, showing you how you can become the HU.

Introduction

A highlight of any major ECKANKAR seminar is the special talk the Living ECK Master gives to the initiates of ECK. Initiates' Meetings get right to the heart of how to follow the path of ECK and become a God-Realized being in this lifetime.

For the first time, Sri Harold's talks from the Initiates' Meetings of the past ten years are now available in book form for the chelas of ECK to read and study.

The thirty-three chapters in this book offer guidance on everyday issues for the spiritual student: how to break out of the rut of habits, get along with others, heal our physical and mental bodies, and recognize inner experiences of the Light and Sound. Most important, they teach the follower of ECK how to evolve into a happier person.

As you read this book, picture yourself in the seminar hall. The HU Chant lingers in the air as the Master walks on stage. The MC announces, "Sri Harold Klemp, the Mahanta, the Living ECK Master." Listen to Sri Harold's quiet voice as he shares his stories and truths with you.

This book holds a wealth of information for any chela in ECK. It is full of the Master's love for all Souls on their way to God.

Part One

Awakening to Spirit

Only love can open the door to the inner worlds.

1
The Purpose of Soul Travel

I'd like to talk about Soul Travel. What is its purpose, and what are the different ways we work with it?

When Paul Twitchell brought out the idea of Soul Travel, he was trying to tell people about this unformed substance called the God stuff, the ECK, or Holy Spirit. He was trying to show people how to become converters of this God stuff.

Converting the God Stuff

When we learn to become a converter of the ECK, it means we have gotten some degree of God Consciousness. This is our goal. We want to bring into our everyday lives the knowledge, wisdom, and understanding of how to become converters of this God stuff.

As we learn to work with the laws that govern this God stuff—which is different from electricity or magnetism—we become masters in our own right. We learn about Soul: What is Soul, what can Soul do, what will Soul not do, and how can we work from Soul awareness? And so we speak about Soul Travel.

Paul spoke about Soul Travel because he was

trying to put into words how to reach this God stuff. He called the process Soul Travel. At first he called it projection, but then people thought Paul must mean astral projection. Astral projection only deals with the Astral Plane, and it really doesn't do anything for someone who wants to reach the unformed God stuff. So Paul made a distinction between Soul Travel and astral projection.

In Soul Travel we learn how to work with this unseen substance—the Voice of God, the Audible Life Stream, the celestial music. We learn how to work with It so that we know our purpose. We no longer run through this life asking, How do I get out of this world alive?

Living in This World

Some people believe it's a mistake that they're here. They try so desperately to get out of this world. They believe life is hard. There's suffering and pain, so God must have got it wrong. What are they saying? They are criticizing God's creation, which includes themselves.

Learning spiritual consciousness is learning how to live in this world no matter what comes. We learn through the Spiritual Exercises of ECK how to live life graciously, from childhood to old age. We learn how to live life in the best way possible.

Some people want eternal youth. Few of us have that mission. What would most of us do with eternal youth? Imagine living forever in the physical body. You may stop aging at thirty, but if your spouse kept aging, you'd have a very unhappy family.

Rather than trying to live forever, we can ask, If not eternal youth, then what's left in life? It's to get such confidence in ourselves through the Spiritual

Exercises of ECK that we know we are Soul, we are eternal. Then we know with certainty that we live forever, that death cannot destroy us.

Strong in ECK

Because Soul's effort to rise in consciousness is above the human level, it is derided, ridiculed, and made fun of. There is much opposition to the ECK teachings by the negative powers. It comes by scorn, by mockery, and by disbelief from the religious and intellectual authorities.

==So if you're going to follow the path of truth, you've got to be strong. And you get strong through the trials of life. As you face each trial, you ask the ECK, "What do I do now?"==

The Light and Sound of ECK is within you. It's not a visitor, not a guest, not a stranger. It's the high consciousness that each of us can reach to some degree, depending on our initiation.

The Second Circle means that our consciousness of the ECK operating in our life has expanded to a certain extent. At the Third Circle we have an even greater understanding of how the laws of ECK work with us and with other people.

If you have any questions about spiritual consciousness, I'd be happy to answer them.

Self-Surrender

Q: What are the steps for a chela to reach self-surrender?

HK: I could give you a list of things, but it'd be a mental understanding. You're never going to get rid of the five passions just with the mind. The spiritual exercises are the key to surrender.

Trust the ECK completely. Until you give up your fears and doubts, you're going to find them barriers to the doors of heaven. Only love can open the door to the inner worlds.

==When you do the spiritual exercises, fill yourself with love and goodwill. Then say, "I now put my inner experience into your hands, Mahanta. Take me wherever is best for my own unfoldment at this particular time."== This will do much toward opening you for self-surrender. It's about doing, not thinking.

What about the Mind?

Q: I try to still the mind and hold the vision of the Inner Master during my spiritual exercises. But I've been disappointed with my inner discipline. Can you reach the high states of the spiritual heavens with the mind still jumping around?

HK: Someone once told me he didn't really look for the Inner Master; he just looked for the Light and Sound. He realized that the Inner Master was just there to help him get to the Light and Sound.

The mind has to be dropped at some point. It doesn't go into the high worlds. But we get panicky. We worry about the mind not staying still, and we start thinking more about whether it is jumping around than we do about the ECK. We believe as long as it keeps jumping, we've failed.

When you get tired of watching and worrying about the play of the mind—when it becomes tiresome, like watching a rabbit or a kangaroo jump around—then you'll begin looking at other things. That's when the mind finally settles down. If you visualize it as a jumping kangaroo, you'll get tired of it and it'll slow down on its own. Then the Inner Master can begin working with you in the dream state.

When We Remember Dreams— and When We Don't

Q: I'm not remembering my dreams as much. I used to write them down every day and was able to see my future very clearly. Of late, it's not as vivid. Why?

HK: You're getting used to that level of initiation. You're coming into harmony with it.

Here's an example: If you drove down the same road every day, pretty soon you wouldn't notice the things you had seen the first time you took that route. Maybe the traffic used to upset you, but now you're an old hand at that road and you just do it.

Also, you don't always remember when something good happens. You'll be having an inner experience with one of the Masters at a Temple of Golden Wisdom, and it'll end sometime in the middle of the night. Still semiconscious, you'll want to continue it. You'll put yourself back into that state of consciousness hoping it'll continue, but it won't. In the meantime you forget what happened.

You have to have the discipline in the middle of the night to say, "This was noteworthy as an experience. I have to make this old body get up, grab a pencil, turn on the light, and write it down, because a better experience won't happen tonight." Discipline puts the idea into your mind that if you want to record anything, you'd better get this one down.

Purification Process

Q: When I was in the hospital, close to translating, I had an experience where I went upward through the higher planes. It was a wonderful experience, frightening as well as beautiful. I felt it was a purification process.

HK: It was. We visit the higher worlds first. If you're a Second Initiate, the Mahanta may take you to the Fifth Plane or higher. This doesn't mean you're a Fifth Initiate. It means you're getting experience: It will help smooth the transition from the Second to one day being established on the Fifth Plane, because you've been there before.

It's done that way on purpose so that you can lead a well-balanced life, to avoid radical changes and upsets.

How to Contemplate

Q: Are there reasons for keeping the back straight in the spiritual exercises?

HK: You can do the spiritual exercises in a number of different ways. Usually, any guidelines I give are to help you develop the self-discipline to remember what's happening on the inner planes.

You can do a spiritual exercise lying down. You can even do one in the car while you're driving to work. It doesn't have to be at night with your eyes closed. It can be in the daytime with your eyes wide open. You may want to experiment and try different methods at different times.

Lying down makes some people lazy, and then they don't remember the inner experiences. But if you're married and your spouse is not an ECKist, it may be better to lie down because when you sit up in bed it can destroy the family harmony. If you're in military housing or a school dormitory, I wouldn't recommend contemplating in the lotus position. You're going to stand out and cause comment. This could create unnecessary problems for you.

Use the spiritual exercise that works best for you based on the outer conditions you're faced with. No matter which one you use, all you really want is experience with the Light and Sound of God. If you have that in the one you're using, then keep doing it.

Can Soul Ever Fall?

Q: Even if we go as high as we're capable of in this lifetime and we have the protection of the Master, is it still possible to fall spiritually?

HK: That all depends on the individual. As long as you're in the lower worlds, it's possible. Whenever you give service down here, you decide to reincarnate in a physical body. You may have made certain spiritual gains in a previous lifetime, but you still have to face life here.

Say a Soul reached Self-Realization in another lifetime, then chose to come back here to serve the SUGMAD. Often the memory of past lives is erased. That person will have to go through the exact same problems as anyone else.

But that Soul will have a deeper knowingness and a restlessness inside to find that special something that's missing. When the time is right the ECK Masters will pull aside the curtain, and that person will begin seeing glimpses of why he came here.

If they let you see the whole reason right away, you wouldn't care about developing the disciplines you need to live in that society at that time. You wouldn't learn the language, the values of the people you live with. And unless you did, you couldn't be as good a vehicle for ECK.

No matter what state of consciousness you've reached, there is no ultimate perfection for anyone. It's an expanding understanding of the laws and ways of Divine Spirit. It never stops. I'm learning, all the time.

Soul-Mate Fallacy

Q: Does the theory of Soul mates still stand? It's in Paul's book *The Three Masks of Gaba.*

HK: Paul wrote that book many years ago. So often we forget that life is a process, not a product. Paul also had to go through the steps of spiritual evolution. He searched the world over when he was looking for answers. One of the occult theories is the Soul-mate idea, and Paul had to come to an understanding of it, too.

At that point, Paul had yet to become the Mahanta. And until he became the Mahanta, there were things he had to learn. One was about reconciling the two forces that come down from the Soul Plane, where the ECK splits into the negative and the positive. It shows up here as the male and the female.

The positive force comes into the male, but it splits up a couple of times into different characteristics, both positive and negative. The negative stream has its positive and negative, too. Thus any individual can have all the positive and negative characteristics. But the point of it all is Soul.

Soul has to grapple with the two streams within Itself in the lower worlds. Some people believe that when they find another person, a Soul mate they can marry, some kind of magical fusion will take place and they can now go to the other worlds. But it's not true. We each are a total unit as Soul. The theory of Soul mates says that Soul can be split. Soul cannot be split.

A Marriage of Souls

Soul has to come into balance with Itself. There's a fusion or merging of the positive and negative forces inside Itself.

When two people who have balanced the two forces within themselves come together and marry in this lifetime, they are like pillars together who stand strong, each individually. And then they help each other in their mission in life, in what they each want to do.

Before someone reaches Self-Realization, a marriage is like two columns leaning against each other for support. If one falls, the other collapses. But once you have Self-Realization, you have total unity and balance of the spiritual self. You are a full, complete unit—a spark of God.

The purpose of Soul is to find happiness where It can because being happy, It is in communication with God.

2
Path to Self-Mastery

The purpose of Soul is to find happiness where It can because being happy, It is in communication with God.

We come into this world as the inexperienced Soul. Because of this inexperience, we haven't learned how to use our free will. So SUGMAD gives us every experience possible to help us learn the wisdom of God. It is here the Inner and Outer Master is of importance.

Looking for a Master

First, we look for a Master. We have looked for and found many masters in the past. Some have been the Outer Master, and some only the Inner Master.

The Outer Master is the one we can see, shake hands with, and listen to at ECK seminars. His duty is to provide ECK books and discourses for everyone who wants to step onto the path to God. He tries to give the spark to Soul and whet Its spiritual appetite so that It will want to return home to God. The Outer Master thus points the way to the Inner Master.

The Inner Master gives the divine wisdom at the inner temple. This, then, is the importance of the ECK initiation. Soul's purpose is to get the linkup with the ECK, the spiritual force.

The Inner Master comes—sometimes in the dream state, other times during contemplation—to give spiritual instruction and to travel with the initiate in the high worlds of ECK.

States of Consciousness

If you have any questions of a spiritual nature that you'd like to ask, I'd be willing to answer them.

Q: What is the relationship between the Mahanta and Jesus Christ?

HK: That's a very good question and one of concern to anyone who has grown up with a Christian background.

Jesus was a man who had a spiritual state of consciousness. This spiritual state of consciousness was called the Christ consciousness. The religions today hardly understand that Jesus the man had the Christ state of consciousness. They often consider it much the same as if *Jesus* is the given name and *Christ* the family name.

The Mahanta is also a spiritual state of consciousness. In past history, the Buddha was a state of spiritual consciousness, as was Krishna. Each came in his time to answer the spiritual needs of the people.

Yet, Soul is a unique entity. This means that each person is at his own level of consciousness. This is the reason that so many different teachings exist within Christianity, Buddhism, and Hinduism, for example. This is the natural order of divine education established by God.

There is a religious teaching to fit every Soul, and so we always respect another's teaching. We respect his religious teaching because it is important for his spiritual unfoldment.

The Living ECK Master and the Mahanta

Q: I want to know the relationship between the Mahanta Consciousness and the consciousness of the Living ECK Master.

HK: Very simply, the Outer Master is the Living ECK Master. The Inner Master is the Mahanta, the ECK of Itself.

Any Living ECK Master who has attained the Mahanta state of spiritual consciousness has truly earned that state. The Mahanta is not a person, but the ECK Itself. Past ECK Masters who still retain the Mahanta Consciousness are spiritual giants like Rebazar Tarzs and Peddar Zaskq.

Depending on your spiritual needs and state of consciousness, the ECK may take the form of any one of these ECK Masters. This is often because you and that particular ECK Master have been together in previous lifetimes.

These ECK Masters are of the Order of the Vairagi. This means they have attained the state of God-Realization and detachment. Their only concern is for your spiritual unfoldment and your return to God.

We are at a great time period in spiritual history. It's the first time in almost five thousand years that ECKANKAR has come into the mainstream of life. The SUGMAD is giving the world an extra spiritual boost.

As We Grow Spiritually

Q: Why does the individual attain the consciousness of Soul at some moments but lose it at other moments?

HK: It's probably due to the inexperience of Soul that I spoke of earlier. It takes great self-discipline to live each moment in the presence of God, so that we may live in a hut the way Rebazar Tarzs does and still be happier than a king in a palace.

If we can learn to be happy, then we are living with the Voice of God.

Working with the Spiritual Exercises

Q: During the spiritual exercises, I have a hard time focusing on the Third Eye. I feel better keeping my eyes open and focusing on the Mahanta. Is this OK?

HK: Always use what works for you. A spiritual technique that works for you today may not work two months from now.

When It unfolds beyond the scope of a particular spiritual exercise, Soul must begin to use the full power of Its creative imagination to find the middle of the great wave of ECK. This continues throughout your spiritual life. You must experiment and look and search. Always trust the Mahanta, for the Master is always with you.

Benefits of HU

Q: I don't understand how chanting HU can bring us the protection and guidance of the Master.

HK: When a person takes the Second Initiation, the Mahanta establishes himself at the Spiritual Eye of the person. Chanting HU, the name of God, opens our acceptance of the Mahanta's protection.

All evils and dangers are really caused by our own negative thoughts. Chanting HU neutralizes the negative thoughts that come through the Spiritual Eye. Thus, the thoughts are purified and no evil can harm us. Attention on the Inner Master is a great spiritual discipline.

To work with this Inner Master, we must act as if everything in our lives depends on our own actions. In other words, we look to ourselves to solve all our own problems. Then, having made this great effort, we will see the hand of help from the ECK.

The Living ECK Master wants to show you the path to self-mastery. As you grow into that state of self-mastery, you become stronger every day. You learn to become the master of your own life.

What Are Dreams, Really?

Q: We hear a lot in ECKANKAR about the importance of dreams. Should we accept our dream experiences as reality?

HK: The Dream Master uses the dream state until you are ready to speak directly to the Inner Master. On the Causal Plane, he uses dreams to work off the karma of the chela. Sometimes a dream will show you a past life that has impact on your life today. The screen of memory is lifted so that you can have a glimpse of that past life.

There are many things that happen in the dream state besides spiritual education. The Dream Master may give you an answer for your health through a symbol. So we must learn to interpret our own dreams.

Sometimes we experience psychic attacks in dreams, but they are possible only because somewhere we have opened ourselves to them. Yet even they strengthen us spiritually.

Darshan

Q: What is the Darshan?

HK: The Darshan may come on the physical as you look at the Living ECK Master. It does not require physical contact. Another Darshan comes to many who have never seen the Outer Master. These fortunate ones receive the Darshan through the dream state from the Mahanta.

I would like to thank you for these very good questions from your heart. The answers can always be found at the inner temple. You have the source, the divine ECK, within your heart. Approach the altar of God with love and humility, and your answers will come when all preparations have been made.

Do your duty to your family, your neighbors, and your government. There is no hurry on the path of ECK.

The monthly initiate report helps you define things for yourself spiritually.

3
Taking Action

An ECK initiate asked me about the monthly initiate report. I told him, "It's a discipline you do for yourself once you become a Second Initiate. You write from the heart. Report exactly what you've seen in your spiritual progress—or lack of it—over the past month."

The initiate report can just be a few lines on a page. It's better if you can keep it to no more than one page. If you have inner contact with the Mahanta, then you don't have to mail it. You can put it on your dresser, next to your bed, or in a drawer. But if you're in any doubt, feel free to send it to me.

It helps you define things for yourself spiritually. It also helps me see on the physical if you're keeping up with the spiritual exercises.

Meeting ECK Masters

My daughter stopped by one day when I was working at my desk. She was about nine years old at the time. "I really want to meet the ECK Masters," she said. "Go ahead and do it," I said. I wanted to get my work done, but she kept walking around the room.

Finally I asked, "You're afraid, aren't you?" She laughed a little and said yes.

"Are you afraid of me?" I asked her. She said no. "Then what's the difference? They're just your friends," I said. She thought about it and said, "If I have a choice, I'd rather not see them now." "Fine," I said. "Any time you want help, they're there, you know. Just call on them."

After a few days, she came to me and said, "I was with the ECK Masters last night." "I bet you were really scared," I teased her. "Not at all," she said. "I like seeing them when I'm asleep." She just doesn't want Rebazar Tarzs appearing behind her in the room.

When we first get into ECK, we can be a little anxious about meeting the ECK Masters. I know. I was, too.

If you have any questions, I'd be happy to answer them.

What Can and Cannot Limit You

Q: Are there any limitations—physical or otherwise—that we must get rid of to become a Higher Initiate and an ECK Master?

HK: Every ECK initiate can reach the higher states. It has nothing to do with physical condition. We aim for spiritual perfection, the higher states of consciousness. Perfection is not something that comes in the physical body.

Unfoldment depends on how much you desire God. But there's a paradox here: If you desire God, IT goes away from you. So you have to have this gentle kind of knowing that you are unfolding, that you are becoming a clear vehicle for SUGMAD. That's what Mastership is.

Who Else Studies ECK?

Q: Is ECKANKAR limited to earth, or is it open to the other planes? Those civilizations that visit us—what do they understand as Spirit? Do they study ECK?

HK: The ECK Masters work with each culture. In our early history, ECKANKAR was submerged. It worked through some of the outer religious teachings. Martin Luther had a little help from the ECK Masters, for example.

The worlds out there mean absolutely nothing until you have your own contact with the inner worlds. Then you can face all challenges and meet with people from other places.

Some of them look at life a little differently than we do. They're not necessarily more unfolded: They just have a different way of looking at life. Some are in an interdimensional phase, like on Venus. They're on the physical plane, but you really don't see them because the vibrations are beyond the human senses. If we went there, we probably wouldn't see anyone.

On the other hand, those on Mars are warlike. That's how they are.

It's hard to say they are spiritually unfolded to this or that degree. It would be like looking at any huge culture, that of the U.S. or Europe, and trying to estimate its spiritual unfoldment. Within each culture you have individuals who stand at the highest and lowest levels.

On earth too we run from the very lowest to the very highest level of spiritual unfoldment. It's true on all planets and all planes. Soul is an individual being that doesn't depend on group association.

Behind government officials stands a line of

masters, and behind this line of masters stand the ECK Masters. They don't let things get too far out of hand, so we're never lost. It's just part of the training of the lower worlds.

Important to Take Action

Q: Since I got my Second Initiation, I've been bothered by a question: What's the best way to be a channel for the ECK?

HK: When a person gets the Second Initiation, the ECK flows in at a certain rate. We set up our habits and patterns so we can give to a degree that balances this inflow. This much comes in; this much goes out.

When too much comes in and it doesn't go out, we become introverted. All kinds of things can go wrong. To avoid this, take action. When you take action, you begin to break free from the pull of the mind.

The Masters want you to take action, to begin doing something in life. You may make wrong decisions. But if it were a choice between sitting still and making a wrong decision, I'd rather you make a wrong decision. At least you learn from it.

When the next initiation comes, more begins to come in spiritually. And in some way you have to give it out. You have to begin to be aware of your role as a clear vehicle for SUGMAD.

The best way to let this flow move out is to do a good deed for someone every day. It may just be holding a door open for someone else.

Facing Karma

Q: Why are the consequences for a person's actions greater at certain times than at others?

HK: Before you get into ECK, you don't see the effects of your actions right away. But as you begin doing the spiritual exercises, the karma, or consequence, comes back a little faster.

We do bad things because we haven't learned some law of Spirit. If we're really stubborn and don't want to learn that law, we create negative karma just from the way we think. The ECK will give us our punishment, and if we don't learn from that, the karma comes back to us a little harder next time. It'll keep doing this until we learn the spiritual law that's behind it.

As we learn a lesson, as we learn to give freedom to others who are also learning lessons, then the lessons become less severe. It's easier on us. Lessons sometimes look harder when we haven't learned, when we're stubborn and won't listen to what Divine Spirit is telling us for our own good.

Everything Depends on You

Q: When a person gets into ECKANKAR, should he try to control his life? If he wants something, should he go out and get it or just allow the ECK to guide him as to where he should go?

HK: Act as if everything depends on you—your goals, everything. Act as if it's all your own responsibility. If you want a better job, sit down and figure out what's going to get you a better job. If you want a house, a car, or something like this, figure out how to get it. But make sure of the things you ask for because you may get them.

This is why it's better to look for the spiritual first: Seek first the kingdom of God, and all things shall be added unto you.

As you do the spiritual exercises, Divine Spirit brings you those things which are for your good, but It offers them very gently. It may be a job opportunity or a love relationship. It's up to you to accept the opportunity.

It doesn't mean that what you get will last forever. It's just there for your experience for a time. Eventually you outgrow it, or it outgrows you. Then you have to find something new. When we work with the ECK, it doesn't mean that life is going to flow on in a constant stream of happiness without problems. It means we constantly adjust ourselves to life as we find it. We take courses, we go to doctors, we do whatever we have to do.

Take action in your life as if everything depends on you. Then leave yourself open for the ECK to help you in those ways you can't help yourself.

Types of Healing

Q: There are many different forms of healing available today. Some seem to be psychic. Are there certain forms to avoid as ECKists?

HK: Many times when people rely on a psychic healer they wait too long. The illness has advanced so much that there's nothing anyone can do. For example, a person goes to a psychic healer, but he only gets a temporary healing. The problem comes back in two, three, or four years. If he had just gone to the proper medical authority in the first place, he might have gotten a real cure.

I usually recommend looking for the best medical help along orthodox lines. Many times it's the most direct. If there's a certain kind that you don't agree with, look for another kind. The decision has to be your own. But psychic healings don't last.

This is the physical plane. Medical doctors are an arm of the ECK. Look for someone who seems pretty healthy, and ask him who his doctor is.

Bringing Back Inner Experiences

Q: When I do my spiritual exercises, I lose track of blocks of time. I believe I'm receiving spiritual training, but how do I bring it back to my consciousness? I'd like to use it.

HK: When we first contact the ECK and experience the things that happen on the inner planes, there could be an imbalance in our daily lives if those experiences were brought back. Until you get a firm foundation, it's a blessing not to know.

Sometimes people get a conscious awareness of the other worlds, and it gives them a feeling of euphoria. They feel so good that they throw everything to the wind—their jobs, their family. They make messes of their lives.

A woman wrote to me about her husband, a medical doctor. In mid-life he got a call from God, or so he believed. Suddenly he wanted to give up his family and his career. This is what can happen when a person is opened up to awareness of the inner worlds without the protection of the ECK Masters.

But something *is* happening during your spiritual exercises. Just let it be. You can train yourself to remember, if you keep a notebook handy. It's hard, but that's what I did. Train yourself to wake up in the middle of the night and write down an experience. As you develop the discipline of remembering inner experiences, you also develop the strength to handle them.

Don't be too concerned about how much you

remember. Pay attention to how the ECK is working in your daily life—just a touch here, a touch there. People can have the most fantastic inner experiences, but if they haven't built a good foundation they fall fast. The first psychic wave that comes along—the first time someone criticizes Paul Twitchell or myself—they get blown off the face of the spiritual earth.

A Little Boost

Life is an adventure. At each seminar you ought to be learning at least one thing to take home with you: something new you can try out, so that you can be a little more in tune with the ECK, so that you can find a little more cheerfulness and happiness in life.

If there is any moment during the day where you need a little boost, declare yourself a vehicle for God. It'll help you through a lot of things. You can get through the biggest things if you go moment by moment.

The teachings of ECK are simply to help you, as an individual, go to the inner source of divine inspiration.

4
Clear Vehicles for Divine Spirit

I often talk about the Sound and Light of Spirit and how It works in our lives. Many of you have this inner contact with Divine Spirit through the Sound and the Light.

The teachings of ECK are simply to help you, as an individual, go to the inner source of divine inspiration. This gives you the spiritual upliftment you've been looking for, perhaps for years.

How We Get Used by ECK

Sometimes Spirit uses us in a way that looks as if we're making a mistake. We're not. We're just doing the best we can, and Spirit uses us.

One night in Singapore, several of us went out to eat at a restaurant. Midway through the meal, one fellow discovered that the car keys were still in the car. And the car was locked. This was the second time it had happened on this trip. The last time it happened, he vowed never to lock his keys in the car again.

He got a coat hanger from the waitress and for nearly an hour struggled to get the car unlocked. The rest of us just sat at the table, leisurely enjoying our meal. We'd been through this before.

In Singapore, it seems that everyone is a friend or a relative of everyone else. An ECKist at our table saw a friend come into the restaurant. "Our keys are locked in the car," the ECKist told this woman. The woman turned to a Chinese family who had also just come into the restaurant. "He can help you," she said, pointing to the Chinese man. The man came over with a big smile on his face. He'd had experience unlocking car doors. In just five minutes the car door was open, and we finished our meal.

The funny thing was, during the previous hour when the fellow was working on the car, he'd gathered a large crowd. He'd met a lot of different people. Spirit will often use us this way to invisibly bring Light to another Soul. We think we've made a big mistake, but that's how Spirit will work through us sometimes.

Lightening the Load of Fear

The ECKist is the ideal citizen of his country. We live and work according to the rules and regulations of our home countries. We work as individuals in a spiritual sense, learning the laws of Spirit that make our lives a little bit easier. They give us understanding, and this takes away the fear of death.

In the Western world, death is of great concern to people. Most religions give no assurance of what happens after we leave the physical body. Having this spiritual understanding of who and what we are is one of the purposes of ECK.

All I want to do is show you how to go within using the Spiritual Exercises of ECK. You can experiment with them on your own. They are a lighter form of going within than meditation.

Let the Light Shine

We do not try to influence people or push ECKANKAR on them; it may not be for them. Each person has an individual approach to God. We just let the light shine from within. People will wonder what we have that is so special. They can tell there's something.

On long trips I like to get some exercise. I like to play Ping Pong, so about nine o'clock one evening we found a community hall that had some tables. They were just closing, but we asked if we could play for a bit.

We got to talking about ECK with several people there and asked if they wanted to read some ECK material. They said sure, so we gave it to them as a kind of thank-you.

This is how we do it; we never push ECK. We let other people be. We give total freedom. If we want freedom, we must give freedom. To get love, you must give love. The same is true of spiritual freedom. You find the more you are able to give, the more you get.

Assurance of the Presence of Spirit

When you put your attention on the Inner Master or you sing one of the sacred sounds of God, it opens you to the love of Divine Spirit. You might get goose bumps or a feeling of warmth that settles on you like a coat. Your face may get flushed. This is the presence of the Master, the protection and love that you have opened yourself to.

Often, before you see the Blue Light or hear one of the sounds, you may have a knowingness and assurance of the Master's presence. I would say a higher way of being in the life of ECK is seeing Spirit at work with you in your daily life.

It's good to go into the other worlds in the dream state. Some people don't do that; others are very good at it. It can give you the assurance during the day that a higher power really has touched you. It will smooth your way throughout the day, if you let It. It will give you confidence and even happiness.

Some people do their spiritual exercises for too long a time. They do them morning and night, for an hour, two hours, three hours. They get too much light coming in. This can speed things up in the physical body faster than it can handle. So take your time.

If you get headaches, that's too much. Back off a little with the spiritual exercises. You could ask on the inner to have it slowed down. I can slow it down. You might also check with a doctor about the headaches. If you're looking for the cause, you'll find it.

What We Learn from Illness

Spirit may give miraculous healings at times. It also may not, because life is here to give us experiences. If an illness is taken away just like that, we may never get an understanding about ourselves. Every illness ought to teach us something we didn't know before.

The purpose of the spiritual path is to bring you a greater understanding of yourself and the spiritual laws. When you get an illness, it may just mean that you have to come to a greater understanding of a spiritual law. As you unfold, even your food habits may have to change. Very gradually, you'll figure it out either by experimenting or by asking a doctor for help. Or maybe you'll read a book and get the answers you need.

Why Surrender?

In ECK, surrender means giving up our fears, our cares, and our worries. We don't give up our money or any of those things; we give up our fears. We do this because we want to become vehicles for Spirit. We want to figure out how ECK can use us, but the fears and cares constrict us and close the connection between Spirit and Soul.

Too many people are looking to use Spirit for material gain. This is not the high path of ECK. Our purpose is to open ourselves as clear vehicles for Divine Spirit. Then It will use us as It wills.

Sometimes we're conscious of how we serve; other times we're not. But what we want to do is come to a conscious awareness of how Spirit is using us, no matter what It brings.

More Than Just a Good Idea

We plan our daily lives; we study if we need to. We may want a better job, better health, or a more compatible mate. But it's not enough to visualize what we want in the mental stream and then sit back and hope it will come. It doesn't work that way. First we visualize it on the inner, but then we set out to do whatever we can to bring that plan into being.

There are many people who have great ideas. Ideas exist by the thousands. The truly rare person is the one who can figure out what he has to do physically to make his dream come true. The inventor has the great idea *and* figures out the technology to accomplish it. It takes work to manifest whatever shows on the inner screen.

Forming a Satsang Class

As an example, if you are interested in giving a Satsang class, first you can send out an inner invitation. Invite people on the inner planes. But then do what you have to do out here to reach people who might be interested. If you give someone an ECK book, you might mention that you have a class beginning.

First send out an invitation on the inner planes. Ask God to bring those people who are ready to hear the message of ECK for the particular class you have in mind. Then do whatever you see is best to form that class. Work with your area leaders.

Go Slowly, Spiritually

When someone first begins on a spiritual path of any kind, they are so enthusiastic. They want to go as fast as they can. But there's really no hurry. When you open yourself to Spirit too fast, you can cause so many problems in your life—money problems, health problems, everything. This is why I generally encourage people to go slowly.

What I'm more concerned about is that you have contact in some way with the Light and Sound, or you see the Living ECK Master in contemplation or in your dreams. This is the ECK manifested as Sound and Light in an inner form. Once you have this contact, the Inner Master will take you at the speed that is right for you. ECK is a lifelong path; it's not something we want to force.

Imagine your life is like a series of interlocking wheels on an old clock. Nowadays clocks are all quartz, and they work much better, but the old clocks have interlocking wheels. If you speed up one part, you upset the whole clock. When you go too fast, it affects not only yourself but your greater circle of life, your business, and the people around you.

We must fit in harmoniously with whatever is around us. Once you are in contact with the higher source, It will take you according to your unfoldment. It's better to be sure and steady than to go really fast and fall back later.

We have some questions here.

Other Ways of Fasting

Q: Is fasting necessary for our spiritual progress? Say I have some stomach trouble. Am I going to have to fast in order to progress spiritually?

HK: When someone's under a doctor's care and on a certain diet, there are other ways of doing the Friday fast than a total fast. You can keep your attention on the Inner Master for twenty-four hours, pulling out all negative thoughts. You can do a spiritual fast.

There are three different categories of fasts. There's a total fast, which means only water for twenty-four hours. There's a partial fast, where you can have one meal, or fruit, or fruit juices. Then there is the mental fast.

Choose the one that suits you. Even this may change. But if you're under the care of a doctor or have a medical problem, by all means take care of the medical problem as you have to. If the doctor says eat, then eat. Or if you yourself feel you should eat, then eat.

Am I Making Progress in ECK?

Q: By the yardsticks given in the ECK literature, I think I am hardly making any progress. In desperation, I have called out for help. Do I have any chance of making progress in the spiritual exercises?

HK: How long have you been in ECK? What yardsticks are you looking for that you feel would indicate progress?

Q: I've been studying the discourses one year. I don't expect something to happen every time I contemplate, but I'd like to see the Light, for example, or even see the Master in my Third Eye. It's difficult enough to hold you in my visualization, let alone see you in my Tisra Til.

HK: Do you remember your dreams?

Q: There was one dream where I saw you.

HK: You're making some progress; you've been in a year, and you're doing well. A year is actually a short time. When I began, I went for two months with nothing; then I had a tremendous experience in the other worlds. Then I didn't have any experiences for months. But I knew there was something happening even though I couldn't remember anything.

Often the Inner Master pulls the curtain because what we would see would be too shocking. I'm concerned about harmony and balance in your outer life— that you don't suddenly do strange things like give up your job, take all your savings out of the bank, and go off to an ashram. That's not the spiritual life.

The spiritual life is carrying out the duties we've adopted: family, children, figuring out ways to support them. This is the challenge in life today.

A Gentle Technique

Some people are very good with the dream state; some are good in contemplation. The dream state is generally the easiest way for the Inner Master to work with Soul, because fears are set aside.

The gentlest technique I know is to say, "Mahanta, I give you permission to take me to that world or that Temple of Golden Wisdom which would be for my benefit." I have used this myself when I ran up against a wall. I'd use it every night before I went to sleep as an inner thought command to give the Inner Master permission to take me to that place I had earned. Then I'd go to sleep and forget about it. The next day I'd see if I remembered something.

Often when we wake up, the inner experience is fresh, but it's so commonplace. We forget it because it's so commonplace. Develop the discipline to write down, immediately upon awakening, whatever happened. If you open that notebook an hour or two later, you'll be quite surprised at what you find written there. More so after a month. Include these dream experiences in your monthly initiate report.

Travel is good because you're in a heightened state of awareness. Everything is strange, different. At home you know you get up at a certain time. You get dressed almost half asleep because you've done it for so many years. You get in the car and go to work. But if someone asked you to describe the third house from the corner on your street, you probably couldn't do it. It's too commonplace. There's nothing to strike the mental screen and make you remember.

It's the same way with the inner; it's so natural that it blends in. The inner and outer blend so much that when you wake up you feel it's not worth the trouble to write anything down. Then by the time you've finished getting dressed, you've forgotten your dream. Just write down a few basic notes to trigger your memory, to give you a key.

This is the point of the monthly initiate report. If you feel you don't have contact with the Inner Master, write it in an initiate report and send it to me. If you are having contact with the Light and Sound and the Inner Master, write the report and ask him whether to mail it. It's simply for your benefit.

Inner experiences don't have to come every day or every moment; that might be too strong for us. It might unbalance us and make us unfit to live among people. If you have contact with Spirit once or twice a month in any way, you're doing all right.

At that point he gives it all to God and says, "I don't know where else to go." In a true sense, this is a kind of humility.

5
When the Chela Is Ready

I'm able to talk more directly with those of you who have been in ECKANKAR for some time. I can talk about things you are concerned about and perhaps explain them. I can help you understand what's happening. We are trying to organize ourselves on all levels, so that there is a conduit or pipeline for the ECK to flow into the worlds with the ECK message.

In the Middle Ages you defended your territory with the sword. These days we do it legally; this is the way we protect our own ground in the twentieth century. Compromises are sometimes needed to open up ECKANKAR so the ECK message can come through in the best possible way. I'd like the least amount of control to come from the ECK Office—but enough so that the message is kept consistent wherever we go.

Working with New Systems

Some of you have mentioned that you don't always get answers from the ECK Office. In administrative matters you ought to. But we have a limited staff, we're setting up new systems, and we continue to add to the study program. Because of this, we don't always have time to write letters.

I have to make sure we grow into these changes carefully and don't take on too much too fast. If we do, we'll find we can't handle it. We'll have to backtrack and do things over. We're going carefully so we can absorb it step-by-step.

Careful Planning

Times have changed, and ECKANKAR has come out into the public eye again. When you're a master with twelve, fifty, or a hundred disciples, you sit at the ashram and life moves at a very easy pace. ECKANKAR has come out into the public eye, and that means we have to have strong ECK leaders.

We have to know exactly what we are doing; we have to plan carefully. Communication is essential for our growth as an ECK community. Today we have the advantage of electronic communication; in a few years the world will be even quicker.

There are some wonderful things happening, and yet behind it all, the message of ECK is still simple. There's always the Master and the individual chela. The teachings are primarily on the inner planes; it has to be that way.

Back in the ashram, there was probably fighting too, even with only a few disciples. One chela was the Master's favorite and had to put up with other people's jealousies. This is just how life is.

The point of ECKANKAR for each person is this: How can I make the connection with the Inner Master? To do this, we have to be able to present the outer teachings. They're not perfect; nothing in this world is or ever will be. But they are the best tool we have to inspire people and show them how to come to the Inner Master.

Rest Periods in ECK

If you have anything you'd like to ask, by all means do.

Q: What does one do if he doesn't want to take the next discourse?

HK: In the new plan, you can take a rest period of up to five years. It gives you time to get your life together, to absorb the ECK teachings, whatever.

If we haven't heard from you after five years, you'll get a letter asking if you're still interested in ECK. If you are, it's time to begin studying again. If you're not, we'll clear the computer of all your records.

This policy gives you a lot of room to regulate your own spiritual life through the guidance of the Inner Master.

I'm also putting pressure on myself to write enough discourses to keep ahead of you, so you won't have to sit on the sidelines and restudy something. I'm working to develop a twenty-five-year study plan in ECK.

Getting Spiritual Training

Q: I often have difficulty with my spiritual exercises. Would it ever be possible to have a workshop on how to do the spiritual exercises?

HK: We've had workshops like this; they're very well attended. People have expressed a real need. They want help with the spiritual exercises, so we will give it. Maybe I'll devote some time in my seminar talks to that.

I want to rekindle the chela's ability to have inner experiences through the spiritual exercises. This is high on my priority list.

The True Realization

Q: Paul says in the *Shariyat* that until we have seen the Master in his radiant form, we have not yet had true realization. Is he referring to Self-Realization or God-Realization? What are the steps to get there?

HK: Self-Realization comes after the Master and the chela have met on the inner planes. The first meeting happens on a subplane of the Astral world, usually during the First Initiation. Some people have a clear visual memory of it, others don't. Even if you don't remember, this is a first step.

The Inner Master isn't always seen as a form right away. Sometimes he appears first as a light—blue or another color. Sometimes he comes like a sound, very gently at first.

A person has to be successful with the spiritual exercises and have self-discipline before he can reach a level of inner achievement. An Olympic contender can dream of winning, but he has to practice. He has to have enough motivation to go out and run every morning.

During the First Initiation, you see the radiant form of the Master. This is not the Self-Realization which happens at the Fifth Plane, but it's an important step in your growth. It is one of the preview steps that has to be taken before you can go further.

Some people don't see much on the inner, but they know that Divine Spirit is working in their lives. You can have inner experiences if you put the effort into it. There are disciplines for remembering your dreams, learning Soul Travel. You can develop these abilities if you try.

When the Chela Is Ready

Q: What is meant by the statement, When the chela is ready the Master will appear? Is there some sort of purity we have to attain first?

HK: It takes a humility that the person himself doesn't know he has. It takes being tired of life—when a person's gone as far as he can, tried every side street, and finally given up. At that point he gives it all to God and says, "I don't know where else to go." In a true sense, this is a kind of humility.

Then the teachings of ECK come slowly into his life, through a book or someone talking to him about ECK. After the first contact is made, the ECK enters his life in a greater and greater way, until finally It has all of him.

People don't really like to hear truth, but through the process of the ECK coming into you, and later beyond the Eighth Initiation, you've given up every part of your person. You've given up every personal desire. Your life becomes one of pure service to Divine Spirit. As you give service with love and willingness, you start to unfold as you never before could have imagined.

But if you don't give up to ECK at this point, It can become ruthless. The destiny of Soul is to become a Coworker with God. One way or another, God will have you.

How God Speaks to Us

Q: How can I shut out the outer noises during a spiritual exercise, to keep from hearing cars and other sounds?

HK: Actually, the outer sounds may not be intrusions. Every so often, one of them may actually be an ECK sound.

Sometimes in initiations I've given, just at the point when the initiation is going to begin, it seems as if every fire truck in the city starts up its sirens. Other initiators have also reported this; some believe it ruins the initiation.

They don't realize that when a spiritual event is taking place in the inner planes, the physical world is going to reflect the enormity of the Sound Current. The physical world is going to raise its pitiful little voice and say, Can you hear the Sound?

Teach the mind not to resist the noises. If you hear honking or people banging a door, just say to yourself, There's a banging door. It may be a message: Spirit is opening a door for you. You grow with the distractions and make them work for you. You laugh at the distractions and start having fun with the spiritual exercises. When you hear a siren, you can say, "The ECK really wants me to pay attention to something." This is how you use negative energies for your benefit.

We are all vehicles for the ECK. Things I'm not able to say, others will say. Or you will say it to another person in my stead. When the time comes, you will know. The Mahanta is using you to reach another person, to give him the same opportunity you once had to contact the Light and Sound of God.

Even though you hold a diploma in your hand and you say, "Now and forever I am a Mahdis," the state of heaven must be rewon every day.

6
Service to Something Greater

You'd be surprised at how much resistance there is to the idea of service in ECK. Perhaps it's my fault for not being able to come up with fresh ideas. Speakers and writers have to come up with fresh ways of saying the same thing—and I'm always looking.

Giving Out What You Receive

Someone asked a staff member what to do in countries where it's hard to give introductory talks. The person replied, "You've got to give back to life in some way. If you can't do intro talks, then talk to a rock!"

As initiates, we are here because we've had a little or a lot of experience with the Light and Sound. It comes into us, and we can do nothing else but give back to life in some way.

The Fire Within

Being a Co-worker with God is talked about in different ways, but the idea is always this: You, in your spiritual evolution, are moving to the point where nothing is more important than living and breathing and moving in ECK. Service is no longer to the self but to something greater, something outside yourself.

As long as you are not doing this, you are still in the lower consciousness. You will never be happy, you will never be fulfilled.

That's because nothing can ever put out the fire that drives you across the face of the earth—looking, searching, questioning, arguing, and bickering. You're not happy because you haven't found the fountain of eternal youth, which is the ECK. You might have an ECK book in your hand, but you haven't the fountain of ECK truth.

The Spirit of the Law

ECK is love, and there is nothing else. Until love comes into the heart of the initiate to replace fear as the motivating factor in his life, he will never catch the spirit of ECK. He will only understand the letter of the law.

The pharisees of the Bible had the letter of the law. They were so right and proper; they made such rules that they suffocated the members of the temple who worked with them. Since the spirit of life wasn't inside of them, they couldn't give it out to others. Their Spiritual Eyes were closed. In ECK, we're looking to open the Spiritual Eye.

Breaking Free

We like to think of freedom the same way a teenager thinks of freedom from his parents. You get really rebellious in the teen years with all these energies stirring inside yourself. You want freedom, you want to go out and taste life, and the only thing standing in your way is your parents. You're ashamed of them. Not always ashamed—in a good ECK home it doesn't have to be that way—but things may be strained anyway.

We are like children looking to break free. We read *The Shariyat,* and it says how the Master takes you to the Fifth Plane and leaves you there. We believe that from this moment we're free to walk alone.

But remember this: If you need to announce to me or anyone that now you walk alone, it's the greatest proof that you really aren't ready to stand alone. You're the only one who doesn't know it.

You'll say, "I want to walk alone now," and the Master says, "Why, sure. Go your way in peace." And you'll walk on the Fifth Plane for a long time, totally happy. There isn't any time there. Your destiny eventually is to become a Co-worker with God, but there's no hurry.

The point is, Will you allow yourself into the greater consciousness or will you stop where you are? Have you continued to grow spiritually, or have you stopped growing?

Rewinning Heaven Every Day

Just because we reach the ECKshar state, we don't necessarily keep it. Even though you hold a diploma in your hand and you say, "Now and forever I am a Mahdis," the state of heaven must be rewon every day. Be assured that you're always going either forward or backward.

We can't really speak of a plus element in the higher worlds. All is of the world of Light. It's down here where the consciousness strikes the Mental body and comes out as our opinions.

Too often, we assume we're always going forward. Then everything goes wrong. It never occurs to us that maybe there's a reason for it.

First Touch of God-Realization

At the Eighth Initiation comes the first touch of God-Realization. During the transition from the Eighth to the Ninth comes the first soft breath of God Consciousness. From the Eighth to the Ninth to the Tenth Plane it's a gradual expansion of consciousness into a greater consciousness.

A person is approached by the Order of the Vairagi to enter into the Order at the Ninth Initiation. This means that he probably won't be put in charge right off. In a hierarchy there are people who do top duties and people who do whatever else has to be done.

It's like the Supreme Court. These are the highest justices in the United States, but the newcomer—man or woman—gets to do the dirty work. Hierarchies are very practical. When you've earned your place at the top, you get all the benefits that come with that place. You take your lessons at the bottom because you need them to get to the top.

Waking Yourself Up

Spiritual education builds solidly on what you are today. Not on your philosophies or what you think, but on what you do. The spiritual life is a life of action. It may be quiet action, but it's action. It's not sitting on the sidelines, cheering for the team. If we do that, are we really growing?

When we're asleep we're about the last ones to know we're asleep. I've had people tell me, "If I ever slip, please let me know." And I say, "Yes, I will," because I do. But they don't hear me when I tell them. It's the funniest thing in the world.

False Problems

When the ECK is trying to tell you something, you get a certain feeling. It haunts you. The Golden-tongued Wisdom is trying to come through and give you some hidden message.

Sometimes the Master will put false problems in front of you. He'll be very patient as you go through them. You may get so caught up in them that you don't realize what's going on for two or three years. Finally you see the futility of your actions; you look back and say, "Now I see the real purpose of that experience."

You may chase yourself to some distant part of the world and back, still not quite sure what your secret mission is. Maybe the mission had nothing to do with the long trip; maybe it had something to do with going inside yourself and getting experience there. Getting a knowingness and greater awareness of your God state.

What Lies Ahead

In *The Shariyat-Ki-Sugmad,* Book Two, it talks about someone ready to receive the Sixth Initiation. If he reads in *The Shariyat* what it takes to become a Sixth, he has to be a pretty strong person to take the initiation. All these things could happen to you.

I generally felt fearful before each initiation, wondering if there would be enough pieces left when it was over to carry on to the next one. But somehow yesterday passed, today came, and tomorrow will come. As a spark of God, a particle of the ECK, we can't be lost in life.

Once in a while we're brought right to the borders of death. We can be as detached as we want, but when we're faced with it, we say, "SUGMAD, not yet!" It's not so much fear as a recognition that we came to earth to fulfill a service to God.

But when you finally leave here, you don't care. You just don't care. The other worlds are beautiful and wonderful. And no matter where we are, we are the active vehicles for Spirit.

Perfect Guidance

We look to the past to give us lessons so that we can make today better, but we don't worry about what the future brings. There's a state bigger than the ECK-Vidya, and that's no longer calling it up. If there's something you need to know, you let the ECK tell you. You let the ECK bring it to your attention.

In other words, you're so infused by Spirit that you let It guide you wherever It will. I'm not saying you sit on your hands. You move forward. You do the best you can.

Sometimes you go through some terrible things. Other people wonder, How did you survive that? Very easily. You followed the guidance of the ECK, and It tiptoed you around the rocks and rough spots. You can come out of disasters in quite good shape.

Degrees of Love

The ECK will bring other initiates to you, as well as people who aren't initiates. Each brings you a part of the secret wisdom. There isn't any one of us who contains it all. We would have to have the absolute highest consciousness, and there is no such thing. Consciousness is ever expanding. As much as we know today, we're still scrambling. The ECK is giving us the potential for a greater vision so that someday we can know the secrets of life the way the great ECK Masters do, such as Rebazar Tarzs.

These Masters have more compassion than we can imagine, because they have put in more time working with people. Fubbi Quantz has the capacity for more love and compassion than I do. Yet it's the nature of the SUGMAD to take the new guy in the Vairagi Order of the Mahanta and give him certain duties—one of which is to be out here working with you. I make no pretense of being infinite in love and compassion, nor do the other Masters. There are always degrees.

Exercising Your Spiritual Option

When you, the initiate, enter a new plane of consciousness, it's an opportunity to unfold to a greater level than you've ever had before. But it's only an opportunity. It's not a right nor a guarantee. It's like an option on a piece of property—you have to exercise it. Unless you act, you lose the option.

Because you have made a commitment to ECK, I can speak more directly to you. This is why I ask that Second Initiates and up be included in these meetings. Those who haven't yet made the commitment to ECK— their time will come when they've earned the right.

It isn't as though we have any secrets here. We really don't. Truth is available to the whole world. The only problem is that most people haven't the eyes or ears to recognize and accept it. The nature of the human consciousness is such that when it comes in contact with truth, it tries to stifle it. It can't help itself.

The ECK and the Kal are diametrically opposed, and we have these two elements in ourselves. They are constantly at war with each other. The only cure for this is the sweet song of our secret word or HU.

By making the effort to be here, you have made another commitment to ECK. You have exercised your option and said to the ECK, "I wish to grow, I wish to take another step." I'm happy that you came to be counted for ECK.

As we grow, ECKists will begin working in traditional service areas, such as hospitals. They'll do this because they want to, just as some ECKists work with youth because they like to.

7
Spiritual Co-workers

An initiate asked me, "How can we present ECK?" He wanted to know if chelas can share it in a more indirect way, instead of always speaking about ECKANKAR. "Can we speak about things that others care about and share ECK at the same time?" he wondered.

"Keep talking about ECK, but make it clear and simple," I told him. "Explain it. If you start saying 'ECK, SUGMAD, Mahanta' to people who don't understand these terms, you're not talking to anyone but yourself."

If you use the word *ECK*, give an equivalent they understand. If you use the word *SUGMAD*, tell them it means God. During introductory talks, use *God* mostly, use *SUGMAD* sometimes. You can even talk about the quality of IT, the Ocean of Love and Mercy.

ECK Outreach

As we grow, ECKists will begin working in traditional service areas, such as hospitals, just like people in other religions do. They'll do this because they want to, just as some ECKists work with youth because they like to. It's important to use the talents and skills you've developed. Then you're working as a channel for the Light and Sound.

As the Light slowly comes on in an area, It always comes through the individual. When Paul was giving out the ECK message in an area, he'd look for someone who really cared about ECK. Then he'd work closely with them, as closely as his time allowed. That one person was a nucleus other people could gravitate toward.

It's very much like the creation of the worlds. First there is an unformed mass, then very slowly other things gravitate toward it. Pretty soon it becomes a body.

Helping Others Across

A hospital administrator in New Zealand works the night shift. She's noted how often people choose to translate, or die, between 3:00 and 5:00 a.m. Often around that time a call would come from one of the nurses, "Could you come down to the floor? Someone's about to die."

Before the translation occurred, this ECKist would try to spend time with the person. Her function was to make the translation from the physical to the inner worlds as smooth as possible.

She doesn't usually use words like *ECK* and *ECKANKAR* when she's dealing with the dying. She talks about ECK principles, but she doesn't use ECK terms. Her area of service takes a lot of courage. People can be in the worst condition possible before leaving earth and going on. They're often very much afraid; they need someone there who knows and understands.

Is Your Religion Helping You?

A man had been a Christian for years. He always followed his inner guidance. One day it said to him, "Go start a peach ranch up in Colorado," so he did. All his neighbors asked him, "Why are you giving up your good job to do such a thing?" And he'd tell them it was his inner guidance that told him to do it.

The peach ranch turned out to be a success. After a few years he received another message to begin a construction business. He sold the peach ranch at a profit just about the time construction boomed.

Because other building contractors didn't want the work, the man began building churches. The other contractors disliked the church committees; the committees took forever to make a decision. It took a man of great patience and tolerance to work with them. This man had both. He created a niche for himself in the industry. The man became a millionaire in several years.

After a time, however, the man became very ill. He'd been fighting a disease for many years, and he'd done a good job overcoming it through different health treatments. In his midsixties it finally caught up with him.

When it came time for him to cross the threshold, the man got very strange. He kept a loaded gun by his bed, and he talked about taking his wife with him when he died. He'd been a born-again Christian, a very staunch believer, but, at the end, all the years in his religion didn't do him a bit of good.

It's very easy to be strong and smart before the day of reckoning comes. But when it arrives, we ask ourselves, "Am I really ready?"

Silent Witnesses

The teachings of ECK fill a great void that exists in today's religious society. People simply aren't getting the answers they need. They go to church, they have garage sales, they have social activities, but they don't have the Light and Sound. This leaves people empty.

As you work for ECK to fill this void, many times you're going to be silent witnesses. People are going to ask you, "What are you? Who are you?" Because as you take your talents out in the world, you'll be living a dual role, your own life and the life of ECK. When the time is right, the right people will come to you and ask you about ECK in a natural way. You won't have to force anyone.

Try to Serve People

If you have any questions, I want to make sure you get your time in.

Q: I started a book discussion class, but then I was told to end it after six weeks because of a new policy. I didn't understand why this was necessary.

HK: I can go into a long explanation of why new policies are implemented. I do when necessary. But a lot of the time people won't understand the reasons behind them. I try to make policies very simple and just hope that someone uses common sense when putting them into practice.

In earlier times, book discussion classes went on for eighteen months. People weren't getting to the ECK discourses, and nothing was happening in their inner lives the way they expected. So they complained.

If we structure a discussion class to run six weeks, it keeps the class fresh. When you get near the end of the six weeks, you begin bridging the gap into the next area. You ask if they would like another book discussion or if they would like to go into a Satsang class.

In other words, you try to serve people. You do it

smoothly, without abruptness.

When a policy comes out, use common sense in implementing it. Don't wait three years before doing anything about it, but you can take a couple of months, if you need it, to make the transition smoother. Instead of doing it all on your own, talk with the Higher Initiates in your area.

You've got to trust ECK, too. Catch the spirit of the six-week policy, and eventually you can work it down to the letter. When the spirit is there, you're going to be operating without fear.

ECK and Drugs Don't Mix

Q: A lot of people who are my age and interested in ECKANKAR are also very heavily involved in drugs. Sometimes it's a problem for me to talk with them about ECK. I want to know how to deal with this.

HK: People think they can get illumination through drugs. But the fact is, they haven't any self-discipline. They're hooked into something they haven't any control over. If they don't have the self-discipline to drop drugs — and it can happen overnight — they certainly won't have enough discipline to stay on the path of ECK.

If you like them as friends, keep them as friends. But I wouldn't encourage them to get into ECK. I'd discourage them, actually. Say, "You'll have a bad problem if you try to mix drugs and ECK. I'm not going to encourage you." Be firm with them; tell them.

You can't compromise with the ECK. Sometimes, because of friendships, we like to compromise our hardline attitudes. That's what friendship is, the give and take on both sides. But if you're going to talk to others about ECK, don't waste your time on people who are still on drugs.

New Forms of Healing

Q: I'm a nurse, and I teach classes using creative visualization and guided imagery. It's not like laying on of hands; it's teaching people to use their own healing energies within their own bodies. People in my classes often want to know more about ECK. But I've been wondering if this type of healing is in conflict with our teachings in ECK.

HK: This is the indirect way of being a Co-worker and serving ECK. You're not sitting there pouring ECKANKAR into their ears. You're just saying, "Here's a creative technique you can use." Explain the principles. They'll put it into practice and find out it works. Pretty soon they'll want to know more.

Kind Words before Translation

Q: I work with people who are getting ready to translate, and I always call on the Mahanta to help them across. Is it all right to do this? And what, if anything, can I say to them?

HK: Sometimes people aren't very conscious. You can talk with them in this way: "If there's any way that I can help, if there's anything I can do, let me know." They may say, "Can you pray for me?" And you say, "Why, sure." Then go ahead and silently do your ECK practices.

Letting Others Learn

Q: Our son is only four, but he is already showing a definite interest in and ability to take on other people's illnesses or hurt. What should I tell him?

HK: Explain the principle behind it, then leave the choices up to him. You can say, "You probably had a past life where you were a healer. This is great. But do you understand that people have their troubles because they've made them for themselves? They use them to grow."

Explain to him that if he takes these troubles on himself, he must make sure it's with their permission. He must do it only if they ask him. Otherwise, he won't be doing them or himself any good. He'll get their sicknesses, and they won't learn their lessons.

If he has this ability—even if he's four—he probably has the intellectual or spiritual ability to understand you. Just explain the consequences of what he is doing, but not in a woebegone way. Let him make up his own mind, because he will. He just needs to be introduced to the results of his actions.

He'll learn how to direct this in another way. He might like healing. But we're in a society where you have to have a certificate or you run up against organizations like the AMA. He may learn how to affiliate himself with people who have these certificates.

In other words, he's going to have to learn how to do whatever he has to do, yet conform to the laws that exist here—both the legal and spiritual laws that govern taking on problems and the injury it can cause to himself.

Healing can be a glamorous thing. If you're really a healer, you get a lot of people following you. You've got an assured income. But you still have to get back to the basics: What is the principle? Soul is on earth to get experiences. That includes your son, as well as the person who is sick.

The process of sickness and the process of healing ourselves is part of the education of Soul. If you have an illness and you come out of it by guess or by golly, you certainly should have learned something. That's what you're on earth for—to learn *something.* That's why a person has problems and illnesses in the first place.

A lot of people just have the consciousness to go to the medicine cabinet and get an aspirin. They never figure out why they're making themselves sick. They take something that gets rid of their symptoms, but in the meantime a bigger illness is growing in them. They're not learning the real reason.

Handling Future Changes

Q: Where do you see ECKANKAR in two or three years?

HK: I see definite, steady growth. We can't grow too fast because we'd outgrow our ability to handle the people who want to come to ECK. But we can have good, solid growth.

We have to establish ECKANKAR as a valid religious teaching. We want to do this in a quiet way, not blast people with an announcement that we're here. The changes over the next few years are going to have deep-seated implications for our future. And this will be seen better probably in twenty-five years, looking back.

We have some big changes coming up. They're good ones, but they're going to upset some people. Some people are going to feel that the changes are wrong; they're going to leave ECK and do other things. But if these changes are made gently enough and people are given the spiritual explanation of why the changes are necessary—why they're part of our growth cycle into the public in this era—the ripples will be smaller.

The individual will be able to accommodate himself to the changes.

We have to build carefully. Right now I'm doing quiet things that are preparing the foundation. I'm putting seeds into the ground.

I feel obligated to report what I'm doing. But how do you explain to someone who doesn't understand the growth cycle that it takes a planted seed six or seven months before any results show? Whenever you set up anything new, you have to watch very carefully and make adjustments.

Mostly I'm following the Law of Silence. You just have to look to the inner. The fact that there is steady growth now is an indication that the ECK is flowing through the ECKANKAR organization as a channel. By the time the changes come, most of you will have gotten wind of them on the inner.

That Was Smooth!

Three years from now some changes will have come, and you may not have even noticed. You might look back and say, "That was smooth!" It's like a man walking toward the horizon. He never reaches it because the world is round, and he just keeps on walking forever.

In some of the arcade games, you fly your jet fighter to the mother ship, and you encounter obstacles. It may seem like forever before you dock. But once you're there, you only take a few minutes' rest before you're out on another mission.

Our true relationship with the ECK is like the relationship between a man and a woman who truly love each other. They do things for each other simply out of love.

8
Riding the Waves of Change

Before we arrived for this seminar, Sydney got nine inches of rain in a twenty-four-hour period. The weathermen couldn't believe it. The rainstorm hit the city once, backed out over the ocean, then hit the city two more times.

The storm slowed up our arrival. Our airplane had to circle so long we put in at the Fiji Islands to refuel. As we took off the captain said in jest, "It's a good thing they took my credit card. I don't stop here much."

When we got here, all the city streets had been washed clean. The air felt really fresh.

When Positive and Negative Meet

An ECKist asked me, "Is there any connection between the seminar being here and this weather?" Whenever there is an ECK presentation of any sort, it causes a conflict between the Kal and the ECK. In the physical it can show up as rainstorms.

In countries where it rains all the time, it has an effect on the people who live there. If you're constantly under a cloud, it's difficult to stay cheerful and happy. It's harder to work peacefully with other people.

The weather is simply a condition of the area. When the Living ECK Master, the representative of the SUGMAD, arrives in an area, there's more spiritual power coming into that area than it's used to.

Right before a seminar, people also have an opportunity to work out their own storms—the ones in themselves and the ones they have with others. This is why ECK seminars are so important for the spiritual unfoldment of ECKists.

Finding Out Who Loves Truth

Wherever the Living ECK Master goes, he finds himself in the midst of many different conditions—physical as well as spiritual conditions. So he reaches out to find those people who love truth to any degree at all.

Among these people are those who think they love truth, and those who really do. People who love truth only a little but think they love truth a lot are very good at the letter of the law. They will be able to quote you *The Shariyat* and its apparent contradictions—where on one page it says one thing and on another it seems to say something else. Those who really love truth put no conditions on truth whatsoever; they love it for itself.

Our true relationship with the ECK is like the relationship between a man and a woman who truly love each other. They do things for each other simply out of love. There are no conditions, explanations, or reasons needed. The gift is given because of love; there it starts, and there it ends.

Once the spirit of truth comes into us, we find our life runs better. We have the patience and tolerance to get along with others and to get along with ourselves.

It all starts on the inside; until it does, you haven't made any gains at all on the path of ECK.

A Practical Life in ECK

If life were all sweet and enjoyable, it would become a dreadful bore. The Living ECK Master faces problems every day of his life. The highest initiates in ECK face problems every day of their lives. Why? Because problems are the material that the ECK gives us to make ourselves greater human beings in the spiritual sense. Not saints, but greater beings.

When the true ECKshar comes to you, your outlook on life is turned right side up for the first time ever. You look at things differently—in a clear and new light. It makes you wonder why you never had the spirit of truth in you before. It's simply because not enough preparation had been done in Soul to allow it to occur. It takes time; it can't happen until everything is ready.

No one can push you in your spiritual unfoldment or make you go faster than you should go. This is why it's not upsetting to me when someone comes on the path of ECK, drinks two cups of the golden nectar of life, and then runs away because it tastes bitter to him.

My principal purpose is to show people how to live a practical life in ECK.

Hearing the Hidden Message

At an initiate's meeting, I am able to talk to you more directly. In the general meetings I speak more in stories. Only an initiate in ECK is able to catch the Golden-tongued Wisdom behind the words, the hidden spiritual meaning of the stories.

As the Living ECK Master I try to present truth in a simple way. I'm always looking for easier and clearer ways to express myself in speech and the written word—so much so that people who just read the surface say, "This is too easy; there's nothing here." Such a person comes to a seminar talk and hears only stories. You need spiritual ears to hear the Golden-tongued Wisdom.

The consciousness of the audience determines what level of truth can be given. The audience is an entity that has a consciousness as definite as any person's. The group encompasses all extremes, but in itself, it is not very quick to understand the spiritual principles, even though individuals in the group may have the ability to hear the ECK-Vidya, the secret truths that the Living ECK Master is giving.

If someone is not ready, he won't hear truth. He's usually looking for someone to talk to him in high, lofty terms; he's looking for God through flowery speech. But the only thing that's going to get him to God-Realization is the diligent practice of the Spiritual Exercises of ECK.

When Waves of Change Come

Spiritual unfoldment never stops. There will always be something that knocks a number of initiates off the path. When Paul Twitchell changed the focus of the teachings of ECKANKAR from himself as a personality to establishing ECKANKAR as a nonprofit organization, it was a shock to some. It was to me. With it came the question, Where is the truth? ECK was a personal thing for me, but I accommodated myself to the change, and life went on. Today no one thinks anything of it.

Right after the World Wide of ECK in 1969, Paul contacted an attorney and set up ECKANKAR as a nonprofit organization. This would protect it in case both he and Gail Twitchell translated at the same time. Paul knew that the ECK teachings wouldn't last if he didn't set up the structure correctly.

The Living ECK Master holds the Rod of ECK Power; he is the SUGMAD's designee. Yet at some point in the time of every Living ECK Master, something comes up that people can't handle. They finally say, "This is not truth," and walk off in a huff. You have to remember the ECK is always in charge of conditions, and they will stay a certain way until the ECK sees fit to change them. The chela has a choice: he can either stay in ECK or leave. If he stays, he becomes a survivor.

People who don't like what they see in ECK may say, "I've had enough of the Light and Sound, and I'm going to get out now" or "I'm going to just tune in to the Light and Sound on the inner until conditions change." They stomp off down the dusty ages, and then finally they come back. All of us have done it in the past; some will do it again. I have no objection. You absolutely cannot get lost in ECK except to separate yourself from the ECK. Then you walk in darkness, loneliness, and misery until one day you earn enough good karma to come into the Mahanta's presence again.

The maturity you've gained since the last storm determines how far you'll go in this lifetime. Some people go very far; others go through one or two initiations and then say, "That's enough." It's a world of imperfection. No matter what happens, there will always be a conflict between the ECK power and the negative power, and people are going to have to make a choice.

The destiny of Soul is to one day become a Coworker with God. Nothing can prevent it, not even the Kal Niranjan. That's why I generally don't fight the Kal Niranjan; there's no need to. He works for the agents of the SUGMAD. Very seldom do I have to override that power.

Aspects of Being a Co-worker

I see you have a question.

Q: I know how to serve the ECK by putting up posters and giving talks. But what do I do with the rest of my day? Am I still serving ECK?

HK: That's a good question. First of all, we're here because we belong here. We can say that all of the lower worlds are illusionary, but the fact is that Soul is here for Its spiritual unfoldment. Through the trials of everyday living, we learn service to God and other divine beings.

One of the jobs of the Living ECK Master is to show people how to take care of their physical health. Another is to show them how to take care of themselves in a financial way. If you take these two elements and apply a third principle—which is an understanding of the spiritual works—you're going to get unfoldment while you're living here every day, serving your fellowman at the same time.

Everything on earth works with the principle, or rule, of threes. Whenever you want to accomplish anything, you have to have the positive, the negative, and the unseen third element.

If you take care of the physical body, it enhances your spiritual unfoldment and your progress toward God-Realization. If you know how to take care of yourself down here, you become a survivor. It doesn't necessarily mean that you're going to be rich. But when you're living the life of ECK, you ought to be able to take care of yourself and be satisfied with your living conditions.

Serving ECK is more than putting up posters and giving talks. What do you do with yourself the rest of the time? Learn how to take care of yourself in business. Learn how to take care of your health. As you unfold you'll have different bodily conditions to take care of. What keeps you a survivor is adjusting as you need to. Keep on with the spiritual exercises, because this is your lifeline to the ECK and the Mahanta. That's where you'll be given the next step you need to take care of yourself.

Cycles in the Lower Worlds

It's foolish to think we'll live forever. It's not the nature of the lower worlds. One of the conditions of the lower worlds is that anything that starts has to end. It's part of the temporal phase of existence—of matter, energy, space, and time.

We can slow the process of aging to a certain degree through the healing methods, principles, and techniques that come to us. We experiment with them. Someone will tell us about a doctor, and we go to that doctor. Or we try another form of nutrition. We try something, it makes us feel better, and we try it some more. We do this until we burn ourselves. Then we back up to cool down, before we take a few more tiny steps forward. As we do this, we're practicing to be survivors. We're practicing randomness, which is the ability to change under adverse conditions.

Develop whatever means you can to stabilize yourself financially and with your health. As you do, you're going to carry the Light of ECK to other people, just by being around them.

Be available to those who want to know more about ECK. But tell them only what they can contain; otherwise you're talking to yourself. Answer their questions, not your own. If you can do this, it will be a great help to me.

Our personal freedom stops where someone else's starts. People forget this. This line—where their freedom stops and another person's begins—is called responsibility.

9
Responsibility and Spiritual Freedom

I went out with some friends the other night to get dinner. We found a nice restaurant with clean white tablecloths. As we sat down, we noticed a man at the next table grumbling to himself.

In front of him was a plate of what looked like king crab. He looked at it and said out loud, "Junk. It's garbage." He created a big scene in front of his date. He said, "I ordered king crab, and it's supposed to be fresh. This isn't fresh." He went down a mental list of all the things that were wrong with the dinner.

Black-coated waiters ran back and forth trying to appease the fellow, but he crossed his arms and simply refused to pay for the food. I was watching carefully. Generally when something this unusual happens, it is a hint from the ECK that the food there is probably not good for me. But I was hungry, cold, and tired, so we ordered. In the end, two of us handled it OK, two of us didn't.

When You Challenge What You Hear

The ECK was trying to tell us through the Golden-tongued Wisdom, "This food's no good." Although It was speaking very strongly, I was tired of jumping up and leaving every place this happened. So were the people with me. Sometimes you go through an experience just to see if what you're hearing is right or wrong.

There's nothing wrong with challenging the directions that the Inner Master, or the ECK, gives you—if you are using it as a learning experience where you are fully conscious of what you are doing. The only sin against Soul is being unconscious of Its acts, of Its behavior. When you're unconscious of what you are doing, you're apt to blame someone else for your troubles.

I sit here today with a stomach that feels like lead, but this is what we do in life: When we feel strong, we trade off for lessons in things we're not sure of. If I hadn't stayed at that restaurant nobody would have known for sure that the food was really bad. So you stay, you eat it, and you take your licks. And you hope there's enough of you left over tomorrow to go out and do what you have to do.

How to Approach Your Lessons

Today we look for truth in our personal experiences. Something told to us doesn't stick as well as something we've actually done ourselves and taken a beating for. Experience is the best way to learn.

Approach your lessons consciously. As you learn and build strength for the next lesson, you can say, OK, I've been good; now I want to learn something else. Then, when the ECK tells you to do something at this speed for this long, you experiment. The ECK says, "Take two weeks," and you say, "I'll try it in one." You push the timetable just to experiment, and this is OK as long as you're doing it consciously.

Initiates look at Higher Initiates and wonder why they still have problems. No one knows everything.

Some of the troubles are caused from unconsciousness, but some of them are caused by fully conscious experimenting in your own worlds. Learn and experiment in your own worlds.

Do you have any questions?

Where Personal Freedom Stops

Q: We can experiment as individuals. But how far can we experiment with the ECKANKAR organization?

HK: Good question. I approach it like this: If a chela has an inner experience that tells him someone else has done something wrong and he wants me to kick this person out of ECK, I generally just forget it. But if a chela tells me, "This person's behavior is such and such," then I listen. Especially if the behavior is hurting others on the path to God.

Our personal freedom stops where someone else's starts. People forget this. This line—where their freedom stops and another person's begins—is called responsibility. It isn't a hard line. In the past, the ECK Office has acted on a report from one person against another, then found out that the person reporting was actually out of balance. So I wait. If a person is really on a bad trip, it will come up again and again. I'll get more than one comment.

Becoming Spiritual Adults

Most initiates are responsible beings at home and in business. But when it comes to the spiritual path, we've been trained to be like children. Most of us don't understand where freedom starts and where it ends. So a chela will do really wild things and wait for someone at the ECK Office to do something about it.

Who's growing in personal responsibility and mastership then? Nobody. How can you grow when the parent is doing it all?

If I don't allow things to take their course, nobody's learning. The cycle is short-circuited. So I generally ask the sensible initiates to talk to the person causing the disturbance. If one person can't get through to him, maybe a couple of people can talk to him. If it's still a problem, then someone writes to the office. I'm taking time because the ECK heals all things. In the process, the initiate sometimes sees that he can't do this sort of thing and expect to move along on the path to God.

A lot of people learn good lessons when things like this happen. The process is more important to me than the product—the product being a pure ECK community. There's never going to be peace in the valley all the time. You're going to have rainy days, too.

Building for the Long Term

Q: Could we start getting a report from the ECK Office that would let us know how many initiates there are, that sort of thing?

HK: These things are nice to know; they would make you feel you are part of a big, strong group. But the numbers aren't important. I'm putting more attention on spiritual unfoldment than organizational size.

We want to make sure our building is spiritually strong, steady, and forward. Because we're building for the long term.

The consciousness of ECK moves on. The individuals who are frozen in a state of consciousness get left behind.

10
A Leap in Consciousness

The bigger seminars no longer allow me to meet with many of you individually; this isn't 1967 or 1968 when the ECK membership was smaller. Times change, ways of doing things change.

Paul Twitchell used to register openly at the hotel and walk around the hallways when ECKANKAR was very young, but he stopped doing that later. The human consciousness was coming in and doing things against the spiritual consciousness. It made it necessary for him to travel more quietly.

Frozen in Time

Early in his career, Paul used the word *bilocation*. Since it was being confused with astral projection, after a while he decided to change it to Soul Travel and the expansion of consciousness. But some ECKists still referred to bilocation. They couldn't make the leap with him.

They were frozen in time and frozen in consciousness. They couldn't follow Paul into the worlds of the expanding ECK; they were left behind. Believing they had the original, true writings, they were sure that even Paul was wrong.

Paul likened it to looking back to your student days at a university. When you were there, a professor might have asked for a term paper on a subject you knew absolutely nothing about. You wrote the paper, and everyone thought it was wonderful. Ten years later—after you have some experience in life—you read the paper again and realize it was terrible, that it didn't have the truth in it at all. You say, "I'm going to have to rewrite this." But when you distribute the revised paper, the same people tell you that the first one was better and truer. Paul was in this position with some of the chelas in ECK.

Keeping Up with ECK

The consciousness of ECK moves on. The individuals who are frozen in a state of consciousness get left behind. They're sure they are right, but they can't make the changes they need to make in order to go forward.

The ECK teachings say that no one can follow a departed Master. But it's interesting to note how many people do cling to a past Master. ECKists who do this think it's OK because his name was Paulji. The only ones who don't know they're frozen in time are the individuals themselves.

Responsibility toward Self

Responsibility toward self applies in spiritual matters as well as health matters. If we learn how to take care of ourselves in simple things, such as our health, it will carry over into our spiritual condition. Taking care of our health is a reflection of our expanded spiritual condition.

Sometimes we turn the responsibility for our health

over to a stranger who sees us for fifteen minutes; who knows nothing about what we eat, drink, or think; and who prescribes medication that gives us a short-term lift. I sometimes question using this as a first recourse, if there are minor things a person could take care of himself.

There are serious illnesses and other illnesses that a person should go to medical doctors for; I do when needed. But since it's my body, I often like to take a chance and try something myself first. If I suffer, it's my pain; but if I get well and feel good, it's my state of well-being, too.

If I can learn what caused the illness rather than have a chemical take it away, I may not get the same illness back with a different mask. I also keep the responsibility for my own well-being rather than put it into someone else's hands.

As our consciousness changes, our health changes. A certain remedy or method we've used in the past probably won't work tomorrow. When you're on a spiritual path such as ECK, your unfoldment moves right along. You're going to find that you constantly look for new ways of healing.

The average person doesn't encounter this: Most people have the same state of consciousness from birth to death. They find a family doctor for life. If the doctor can heal you, it's curable; if not, it's in the hands of God. That's how a fixed state of consciousness works.

Being Spiritually Fluid

The inner link is the edge you have over a fixed state of consciousness. But it takes discipline, the discipline to keep doing the spiritual exercises even when you can't see anything happening.

If you do the spiritual exercises and stay open to the direction of the ECK, you'll be shown the healer or method of healing that is correct for you at this level of unfoldment. This is why the spiritual exercises are so important: They keep the link open between you and the Mahanta.

A year or two may go by that you don't have any experiences, so you might decide not to do the spiritual exercises anymore. Then things go wrong everywhere, so badly that you don't even have time to figure out where all these problems came from.

The reason nothing appears to happen is due to the law that governs activity cycles and rest cycles. You may begin an activity cycle where your dreams and Soul Travel experiences are vivid. Then you go into a rest cycle where you simply have to trust the ECK. This is when you can learn to see the manifestations of ECK in little things in daily life.

I've put a lot of attention on things of daily life because there is a need right now among the initiates of ECK to learn to live in this world. If you can't learn to live here, you can't learn to live anywhere. You can't have the higher states of consciousness until you make your peace with this world.

The two go together, the physical and the spiritual. They can't be separated.

Gaining Confidence, Losing Fear

When you get the confidence that you can take care of yourself here on earth in one small area, you lose the fear that prevents you from Soul Travel or experiences in the dream state. Fear holds us back in every department of our lives.

The basic steps are always the same. The Master

takes us from the outer conditions where he finds us into the preliminary worlds of God—the Sun and Moon worlds. Then he takes us into the pure Astral planes, and upward.

Many of you are advanced students of ECK who can help me with this work. You're strong enough to help with the wave of chelas that is coming right behind you. You become the teachers of those who have yet to learn the rudiments of ECK.

If you have any questions, I'd be happy to answer them.

Good Guidance

Q: I've had trouble in the past working with guidelines from the ECK Office. Everybody in our area would have a different interpretation. I'd like to hear what you have to say about guidelines.

HK: Generally speaking, I like to decentralize. In the past, there got to be so many rules that no one could keep up with them. Something would be published in the *Mystic World,* then something different would come out in the next issue. The body of ECKists sat down like a frustrated pig. They were being pulled here and pulled there, and finally they said, "We can't figure this thing out."

When I speak of decentralizing, it doesn't mean each area does exactly what it wants. It doesn't mean confusion and chaos. Then we wouldn't be able to use the body of ECK to get the ECK message out. There would just be a series of closed channels running against each other.

We are now getting together the basic principles — what is important for us as an ECK organization. I'd like to have most of the work done in the local areas according to clear, simple guidelines from the ECK Office. You know the conditions in your area better than anyone.

Is It Really ECK?

Q: When you have an innovative idea that you feel comes directly from the ECK, but others in your area don't like it, what do you do?

HK: Generally you have to work with the Higher Initiates in your area. They are the gatekeepers of the high worlds, and they are the ones to see whether the idea is appropriate in your area. If you get an urge that you feel comes directly from the ECK, the Higher Initiates will double-check it.

Many of these impulses are good, but you'd be surprised how many are not good. Someone has to be there and look at it carefully. Even though it comes from the heart, it may not be coming straight from the ECK. It may be coming from somewhere else.

Why People Have Problems

Q: What is ECK doing about the sick people of the world? Paul mentioned a time being put aside later in his mission for people with drug problems or mental illness.

HK: Much of this healing has to be done on the inner planes. Understand first that drug problems and mental illness are generally caused by the people themselves. Many people who reincarnated from Atlantis had misused the energies and fallen into black magic; many are paying a karmic debt today. Not everyone, but many. There are very good government and private institutions to take care of this.

If you want to help out privately, this is fine. The ECKist can go out into the world and help where he has a special calling. You may have an interest in this area. But don't become a person who believes that somehow an injustice has been done, that these people are being overlooked by divine forces. It isn't true. Anyone who's on earth has problems. That's why we're here: To overcome the spiritual immaturity which causes all the strife and discontent among people.

I've worked with some of the people on drugs. They easily fall back into the habit because the mind is so strong and their self-discipline so weak. It's better if I work inwardly with them, and with the help of initiates who wish to devote their time to this as a special cause. I appreciate the help.

Although there are ECKists who specialize in working with people on drugs or people who have mental problems, we don't do it as a general program of ECKANKAR. Outwardly I work mostly with people who have worked out more of their basic karma and are closer to understanding the higher truths of ECK.

Part Two

Following Your Dream

One day he remembered to ask for help from the Mahanta and got the inner nudge to take up roller-skating.

11
Following Your Dream

An individual joined ECK, and after he had been in for a while, he slipped away from doing the spiritual exercises. Over a period of time he noticed that everything in his life got harder. One day he remembered to ask for help from the Mahanta and got the inner nudge to take up roller-skating.

He skated at night along a street lined with streetlights. After a few months of skating, he began to notice a peculiar phenomenon. Every time he skated past a particular corner, the streetlight dimmed. When he saw other skaters he asked, "Have you seen that strange light over there? Every time you go past it, it dims." But no one knew what he was talking about.

Then something occurred to him. My life is hard, he thought. I wonder if this has anything to do with my spiritual light?

He took careful note of the streetlight, and sure enough, it dimmed as he passed it. So he got another nudge: to begin the spiritual exercises again, and chant as he skated. Now as he came past the light, it stayed bright. He experimented. When he forgot to do the spiritual exercises for a few days, a whole bank of streetlights would dim as he skated past. But when he began the spiritual exercises again, he found that the lights maintained their brightness.

This story is a graphic example of the manifesting power of the ECK. Down here, It even affects electricity. This story shows the importance of the spiritual exercises for us all.

The Mapmaker

We're moving the ECK Office from Menlo Park, California, to Minneapolis, Minnesota, next summer—that's in July of 1986. Land in the San Francisco Bay Area is very sought after. And as soon as we leave our current building, the owner will be tearing it down to make way for a larger, multi-storied office complex. The earth is erased. It's a phenomenon I call the mapmaker.

In my mind I have this playful image. I see an agent of the Kal hunched over an artist's drafting board in a little second-floor apartment. I call him the mapmaker. His job is to erase locations and buildings from the memories of all people.

People walk by, look at an empty lot, and remark to each other, "Wasn't there something on that lot?" "I don't remember," someone else would say. I think that's going to happen with the ECK Office when we leave California.

It's a good reminder about the lower worlds. Nothing is permanent, so don't get too attached to any buildings. Anything you can see or touch here is subject to change. If it can come and go, it will go. Forms aren't important at all. It's the life that comes to individuals through this outer form, the Sound and Light. This is what's important.

Finding Our New Home

Back in 1980 we put out a big search for property. The Living ECK Master sent out a questionnaire to High Initiates asking their preferences on a location for the ECK Office. I went into contemplation and looked at the ECK-Vidya. It said Minnesota.

When I mentioned it at the time to those in the office, mine was the most far-out suggestion of anybody's. Everyone else wanted exotic places like Hawaii. Nice comfortable places. Minnesota seemed like quite a joke. But that's what I saw. When you see something like this, sometimes you have to follow it out.

First we have to establish our office in Minnesota, then the Seat of Power will be moved from Sedona. I'm moving it for several reasons. In the past there have been a number of psychic forces hovering around the site. We've also had to consider the political situation in South America which is going to push people north into overpopulated Mexico, then into the southwestern United States.

It looks like it'll take five years before we can build on the property we've bought as a home for ECKANKAR. There's a lot of resistance from the people in the area. First they have to get to know us. They have to see we are good neighbors, just as we were good neighbors in California.

Rugged Makes Hardy

I always thought the weathermen in California had it easy. It's the land of two seasons—rain and no rain. If it's the rainy season, they predict a 50 percent chance of showers. They think, How wrong can we be with 50 percent? And when it's the dry season, they say, "It'll be hot and dry today," and give a temperature range from 60 to 100 degrees.

Every so often when a shower comes during the dry season, it causes a big commotion. All the weathermen are caught off-guard.

We're moving from the land of two seasons to the land of many seasons, where the weathermen work with thunderstorms, snowstorms, tornadoes, and once in a while a clear day. I think the move will make the ECK staff hardy. A lot of strong, sane people live in Minnesota.

Most ECK monasteries aren't in tropical climates. They are in cold mountain areas, and the people who live there are pretty rugged. You have to be. So I think this move will be good for us.

My job as the Mahanta, the Living ECK Master is to look for Souls who are awake or are awakening. I try to wake up the rest enough to be ready for the next trip.

12

The Mission of Soul

Sometimes we forget that Soul's only mission is to find out where It came from and where It is going. So often the requirements of just getting along with other people can push in and close out the light of Soul. Soul's search for God can get covered up by the things of everyday living.

Soul can spend a whole lifetime attending to these problems. Every time somebody throws It a rope from the lifeboat, Soul may grab for it. But It finds it takes work to pull Itself toward the boat. It's easier to just sink under the waves and let things be.

My job as the Mahanta, the Living ECK Master is to look for Souls who are awake or are awakening. I try to wake up the rest enough to be ready for the next trip.

Coloring Pictures

When I was six years old, a teacher gave me a picture to color. It was a drawing of grass, big trees, and a sky with fluffy clouds. I was supposed to color each the right shade, but I only got six crayons to use.

I looked outside at the grass, trying to decide which crayon to use. I couldn't find the color in the crayon box that looked like the grass outside. There were so many colors in the grass, not just the color of the crayon labeled "green."

One of my little friends stepped in at this point: "Use this color; it's called green even though it doesn't look like the lawn. Use it, or the teacher will get mad at you." So I colored my picture the way my friend told me to.

We may be pretty good at figuring out which color to use to get along. Sometimes it's the little things we're good at.

Moving to a New Level

Most of you may not remember grade school. Each fall you go to a new classroom. Sometimes you don't have any friends. You're afraid to leave the classroom you're in because you don't know what's going to happen at the next level.

My daughter was really worried about this when she was nine years old. She was supposed to transfer to another school for the next grade. She quizzed me, "Dad, will I have any friends there?" "Half of your friends are coming with you," I said. "What about the ones that aren't?" she said. "You'll make new ones," I said.

Even when you're afraid to leave here because you don't know what will happen next, remember that you'll make new friends. This is what Soul does too.

Spiritual Eyesight

A person attending his class reunion remarked that the people he knew long ago look pretty strange to him now. He felt that he looked just the way he'd always looked, but time had somehow played a trick on everybody else.

He had a tendency to judge people by what he knew of them back in school. This is what we're trying to break out of as Soul. We're trying to look at others with spiritual eyesight and see the Light of God in each person.

People in the human consciousness put limitations on the higher states, such as God Consciousness. Someone who's unhappy will look at another person who's happy and think they're unhappy. He puts all his unhappiness on the other person.

What I'm saying is this: Just because you get into the higher states of consciousness like the ECKshar state, don't expect people to roll out the red carpet for you. They won't. They're looking at you through their own eyes and their own state of consciousness. If you're happy and they're not, they're going to try to make you unhappy. They'll see that you're not rich, and they'll say, "What good is the message of ECK if it doesn't give you material things?"

The further you go, the greater the resistance to things you do. But you have more strength to meet the difficult times. Maybe the happy times are shorter, but they're better. Soul is learning survival. It's learning how to get by in all worlds in all conditions at all times. This is so that no matter where It is, It can survive without being broken to pieces.

Do you have any questions?

What Is the Blue Star?

Q: Sometimes I see the Blue Star of ECK, but I'm not sure if it means I'm doing something right or doing it wrong.

HK: The Blue Star is to make you aware of a particular experience. It is the Mahanta, another manifestation of the ECK. It's telling you to be aware—note this experience well. You won't have to go through it again unless Soul becomes unconscious and forgets.

The Blue Star of the Mahanta may tell you something is a key lesson and give you a warning so you don't have to go through it again. Or It may come as a blessing to help you in all aspects of your life. It comes both ways.

If It tells you about a particular healing, it just means the healing is for you—not necessarily for anyone else. We often make this mistake: If it's right for us, we think it must be right for everyone. We try to convert everyone to what we have found at this particular stage. In another couple of months, we'll probably move on to the next stage.

Keeping ECKANKAR Current

Q: Why are you editing the books and discourses now?

HK: Times change. The way people understand things changes as the consciousness is raised. Material from the 1940s might not make sense today; you might not be interested in the issues.

It's been many years since Paul Twitchell's translation. Consciousness is changing fast because the karmic pace has sped up. People feel and think differently. For example, fifteen years ago you couldn't buy a calculator like I have on my watch.

In the sixties people never talked about being out of the body. It was considered too strange. Nowadays on television I see nicely done programs on out-of-body experiences. People may not accept it, but at least it's part of today's consciousness. Today people are interested in spirituality from a different angle. This is what we address in ECKANKAR.

Leave the Past in the Past

We have to be careful that we don't get tied to the words of the past. As soon as ECKANKAR puts more attention on a past Master than on the present Living ECK Master, then we've become an orthodox religion and are spiritually dead. This is what we have to keep in mind.

The Shariyat we have here isn't the real thing—it's like a *Reader's Digest* condensed version of the real thing. The Shariyat on the higher planes is a living thing of the Light and Sound which translates into huge books on the lower planes.

There are some ECKists who say that Paul's writings were the original word of ECK. They are not moving with the consciousness of ECK. It is always expanding, but they've become locked in time. It's a very sad thing.

A Spiritual Pace for Learning

People have asked me to put all the discourses into a book. Some of them want a book that will magically solve all their problems. I can't give you that.

Soul unfolds slowly, and the discourses are paced to that unfoldment. The different discourses are at different vibrational levels. The words give the inner preparation so that you have success with the techniques.

Unfoldment builds; you can't just throw it at someone. We can't move any faster than the unfoldment of Soul or the group consciousness at the time.

Meeting Other Masters

Q: What is the function of other masters?

HK: Most of us are under the care of one or more masters before we come to ECKANKAR. The first master turns you over to the next master and so on. Then you encounter one whose function is to turn you over to the present Living ECK Master. It's a very natural process.

The path of ECK is the path of personal experience. We learn to listen to our own experience more than to other masters or other people.

The Living ECK Master is the Wayshower, the Light Giver. All he wants to do is light the light of Soul. Then Soul goes out into the world and begins getting full, conscious experiences.

When Soul Chooses to Leave

Q: My daughter was killed in an airplane accident in October. Can you tell me if she's all right? She's not in ECKANKAR.

HK: She's all right. Her instruction goes on. Even when we leave this plane, it's usually a conscious decision of Soul. If you want to meet with your loved ones, you can. Sometimes you'll think it's a dream, but you'll meet with them from time to time.

Soul usually knows beforehand when it's time to go. We can't always see the factors that have brought Soul to that decision. This is why the human consciousness is unhappy. Even as you go into higher states, you still have problems and troubles, but you can now be aware of what is happening and why.

There is no last word on health. People are constantly evolving, and so are their situations. They have to open themselves to the ECK and find the next step in their physical healing. They ask themselves, What do I need now for spiritual healing, for my spiritual growth and unfoldment?

13
Year of Spiritual Healing

In parts of Africa the initiates have a very interesting way of presenting the ECK teachings. The ECK leader in one area is the chief of a tribe of five thousand people; he's also a successful businessman. He tells the chelas to read the ECK works. They're supposed to know them completely.

When a seminar is given and ECKists arrive at the hall, they're asked if they'd like to give a talk on this or that topic. It means they have to be really filled with ECK and know what they're talking about. Most of the chelas in America would be scared to go to such a seminar, I think. But that region of Africa is thriving.

It forces those chelas to rely upon their creative resources. They have to respond instantly. They're not afraid to use ECK terms like *SUGMAD*. But each culture is different, and we do what we have to do according to the needs at home.

Healing as You Evolve

This is the Year of Spiritual Healing, and we have worked to revise *Herbs: The Magic Healers*. There is new information in it from an herbalist, but that doesn't mean it's the last word on health. There is no last word on health. Paul didn't have it, the AMA doesn't have it. People are constantly evolving, and so are their situations.

Some of the herbs of the past won't heal the diseases occurring today. An herbal program you are on today may work for you and no one else; it probably won't even work for you in two or three years if you are unfolding.

The body develops a sort of allergy to a certain series of things if done too often. Some ECKists get on a program and feel it's the only program that will ever help them. During the cycle they're in, they follow it wholeheartedly. But if they're unfolding, pretty soon the body no longer tolerates certain vitamins. They can just feel these things no longer working. So what do they do?

They find something else. The products are still good, but they have somehow outgrown them. Now they have to open themselves to the ECK again and find the next step in their physical healing. They ask themselves, What do I need now for spiritual healing, for my spiritual growth and unfoldment?

Even within a family, different members may need different health programs or different amounts of exercise. One time I went to a chiropractor and told him my back was out. He asked, "How did it happen?" I didn't want to tell him, but he persisted. "OK," I said, "I was doing somersaults on the floor for my daughter." He said, "No wonder. You're too old for them." Children need different amounts of exercise than adults.

Life in ECK is a very iffy thing. It's not a secure life at all. If there were a universal health program I could recommend, such as so much fasting, eating certain foods, or taking vitamin C, I'd certainly give it to you.

Trying Something New

I've known for a while now that I need to exercise more. I get out for walks several times a week, but I'm not in condition to play softball. I have to weigh my priorities, though. I ask myself, Is this a particular time in my life when the thing I want to do most is play softball? No, I'm enjoying writing now.

As you do new things, you ought to be growing and learning. You ought to be trying things you haven't done before. So I'm doing a different kind of writing than I've ever done. A reader might not notice, but another writer might. One chela wrote me that she'd read a discourse and noticed how much work it takes to write each chapter. In my full schedule, actually I get one Saturday a month—and it takes all day. And I usually end up editing it the next day. But I've let the material go around in my head for a month before I put the discourse down on paper. During this whole time I'm writing other articles and other materials that need to be written or edited.

I'm always learning about the wonderful field of writing. I look at people who write well—the Louis L'Amours and the John D. MacDonalds. I like seeing how they go about it. But to be in ECK you don't have to be a writer; just do whatever you do, well.

It's time that initiates take responsibility for their own health wherever they can. But if what you're doing doesn't work, if you've done everything you can, then go to a doctor.

Practice Discrimination

I recently wrote a Wisdom Note about not using the ECK fellowship to make a living selling your brand of vitamins or other products. Don't hand out your business card at ECK seminars. You're not going to make it in business if you have to rely on other ECKists at a spiritual function to promote your business. So save yourself a lot of hardship, and just don't do it.

For the most part I got good responses to the article. But a few people were very upset. Was I defending the AMA? they wanted to know. I'm not defending anyone. But even the doctors licensed in this country are subject to lawsuit. If you're going to push your products, be very careful of what you're doing. Some people are practicing medicine without a license, and these are litigious times.

Once you get in hot water, you're in it by yourself. Out here, I'm nowhere nearby—only as the Mahanta. If you don't listen to the outer warnings, then you have to run the cycle. There's nothing anyone can do to help.

Medical healers are very necessary. If you've allowed yourself to get into such a state where an illness has gotten acute, you need to get help. If you're not smart enough to go get the help when Spirit urges you, then you're going to learn things the hard way. But I don't think it's necessary.

We don't want to get into the position of some of the religious groups who believe all healing comes from the inside and end up in court when a child dies. All healing is from Divine Spirit, the ECK, but It works through outer channels too.

Finishing Cycles You Begin

Do you have any questions?

Q: I had a question about the new RESA program which will be in effect in October. Should we continue with our current plans for a regional seminar?

HK: Life goes on. There are usually overlaps with big projects. Usually when I've set an event in motion, like a regional seminar, I don't stop it unless there is a drastic reason. I carry on. I let the energy that has been started run its course.

Otherwise it would be like rolling a bowling ball halfway down a lane, then deciding you're bowling in the wrong lane. You run after the ball and try to give it a swift kick into the next lane. If I decide I'm in the wrong lane, I say, "OK, so maybe I'll get a strike."

Sacredness of Initiate Reports

Q: Harold, are you the only one who reads initiate reports?

HK: Do you mean, Do I read them myself? I have a few trusted people to help me. The people I've selected have almost given a blood bond.

The initiate reports are so important I have them sorted into categories. I ask to see a certain category of problems, or certain spiritual experiences. The stack of mail from initiates is just one bit of the mail I handle, and I have to get administrative help. Otherwise I couldn't deal with more than a hundred chelas in this lifetime.

But the people who are reading them are very carefully selected. No one outside the circle knows who's doing it. I haven't found a breach yet. They are instructed carefully in the sacredness of the communication between the initiate and the Master. To me it's such a trust that if someone violates it, it's a matter of firing. I feel very strongly about it.

I think you'll enjoy this coming Year of Spiritual Healing. It's healing on a wide, wide basis.

The old farmers back home always smoked pipes. As kids we wanted to try the pipe, but they'd look up and say, "It'll make you sick." They didn't tell us not to do it; they just gave information.

14
Your Freedom of Choice

I caught a train the other day in Holland. I had only two minutes to buy my ticket. Not being used to the first- and second-class system, I just bought a second-class ticket and took the first open seat I saw.

Soon the conductor came along checking tickets. I proudly showed him mine. He looked at the ticket, pointed to my seat, and said, "This is first class." Then he pointed to my ticket, "This is second class." He wasn't really scolding me, he was just giving information.

"Where's second class?" I asked. "Next car." He watched as I got up and went into the next car. When he was sure I was seated, he looked calm and satisfied, then went about his business.

How We Learn to Make Choices

He reminded me of country people on the farm where I grew up. Very seldom would they tell you if you did something wrong. They just told you what was expected, the way a good schoolteacher will do, or the way I sometimes do with the ECK chela.

The old farmers back home always smoked pipes. As kids we wanted to try the pipe, but they'd look up and say, "It'll make you sick." They didn't tell us not to do it, they just gave information.

One time my uncle gave me a puff on his cigar. He enjoyed teasing us; he'd say, "It's easy, just suck in and breathe deeply." I was about five years old. I breathed in deeply, then ran outside still holding my breath. Once I was outside I let my breath out—and everything else too.

Often the Mahanta, the Living ECK Master works with the ECK initiate in this way. He says, "This is expected" or "that is not to be done." Then the individual is given a choice to do what he wants to do. Soul is here to get experience, and many people will try something out to find out why it is not to be done. You can get a lot of experience that way.

The Best-Laid Plans

We make our plans, we do the best we can. But no matter how well we plan, we find that the ECK changes things to make them come out right. An example of this happened to some of the ECKANKAR Office staff en route to this seminar.

Careful arrangements were made to get everyone on certain flights out of New York. But a series of severe storms hit just as we were leaving—a tornado even went through our area. Quite a few people who were supposed to be in New York by a certain time were still on the ground in Minnesota. People who were supposed to fly to Amsterdam ended up in Frankfurt. Others ended up circling over Chicago. We all got here, but not together. If group planning doesn't work, then you try to do it right yourself.

Using the Creative Insight of Soul

Someone from a country in the South Pacific asked me about an ECK-Vidya reading. They wanted to move to the United States. But when they heard that ECKANKAR was moving from California to Minnesota, they put their plans on hold. They asked me, "Would you please advise us what to do next?" I always suggest going to the Inner Master.

Even with the ECK-Vidya, it's better to plan your own life with the Inner Master than try to use an outer guide. The ECK has given you many creative ways to figure out the direction of your life. The ECK has given you a good mind, but more than that It has given you the creative insight of Soul working with the Light and Sound. Soul can put the pieces together.

When you have to make a decision, put the facts on the table, just like you're working with the pieces of a puzzle. You look at them and say, "I have these pieces, but I am missing those pieces." You ask yourself what information you still need to make your plans come true.

Someone might think, Once I get an ECK-Vidya reading I will have no more anxieties in life. This isn't exactly true. By giving an ECK-Vidya reading I would be doing him a disservice. I would have limited the person's creative ability by short-circuiting his connection with the Inner Master and making him lean on the Outer Master.

Advice Is a Funny Thing

So often I find it's better for me to work as the Inner Master with the ECK initiates than as the Outer Master. Advice is a funny thing; you may have noticed it too. Someone will ask you for advice, and as soon as you give it, they say, "No, I can't do that." Then they ask you, "What else can I do?" You suggest something else. They say, "That won't work either." By the third time they ask what they should do, only a fool would say.

People may ask you for advice, you give it, then they ignore it. Pretty soon your feelings are hurt, but you're smarter. The lesson is clear. If you can just run your own life, you will have done well in this lifetime.

In my position as Living ECK Master, I might say, "No, I can't give you advice on your life." But the inner part, the Inner Master, always says, "Sure, I'll give you advice. But you can take it or leave it."

Life comes up to us like the conductor on the train. It tells us, "Something is not in agreement here." It gives us information: This is first class, your ticket is for second class. Unless we are very slow, we should be able to figure out what's going on.

This is the way the old farmers worked at home. When the child asked to smoke the pipe, the old men told him it would make him sick. But the child said, "I'd like to try it anyway because you are smoking it and I want to be a man just like you." Then the old men would give the pipe to the child and say, "OK, be just like us." And the boy learned.

The Inner Master essentially does this too. He says, "Do you want to be God-Realized? Then I recommend you do this, act this way." The chela says, "But I want to act this other way." The Master says, "I strongly recommend against it, but if you want God-Realization, do as you will. You will learn better by experience than by lecture." And the chela does what he wants, then runs outside to take care of some necessities.

Practicing the Spiritual Exercises

I'd be willing to answer a few questions now.

Q: There are so many spiritual exercises in ECKANKAR. Is it better to try many or to stick with one until it works?

HK: Each of the twelve discourses in a series will generally have one spiritual exercise. When you're reading a discourse for that month, do that month's exercise. Next month if there's a new exercise, use the new one. If it doesn't have one, choose one from the past that you would like to use.

When Love Is Missing

Q: Thank you for the change you have brought into my life. There's just one thing missing, and that is for a female to share my life. I feel all these wonderful experiences would be nicer shared with someone. Yet when I look for someone, it never works out.

HK: This is a question many people have. It's the question of love. You can do many different things, you can have the world at your feet, but unless you have love you have nothing.

You may be making money, getting promotions in your company, traveling—but there's no reason for it unless somehow you have love. This is actually Soul seeking God, which It then expresses through human love with a companion.

As the Inner Master I can say that a way will be opened. Often we have to make changes inside ourselves to have love.

Nurturing What We Love

Everyone has some experience with love—even a child who has a pet kitten or a dog. Soul is trying to give back or respond to the love of ECK that's coming through. In some way the child learns lessons about caring for the pet. If he neglects the pet and it runs away, the child learns one of the first hard lessons about love: If you love something, you have to nurture it.

Like anything else, you have to put your full attention on it. Sometimes in the courting stage, a couple focuses all their attention on each other, but after they are married they begin to take each other for granted. Instead of looking at each other when they talk, their eyes drift. Maybe the man is thinking about work, and she is thinking about things happening in her life. They talk past each other.

During courtship when two people are looking at each other very directly, there's the power of love in the gaze of one human being upon his beloved. They can actually feel the power in it. But later when the partners become distracted and put their attention a foot above each other's head, the nourishing power of love, or the ECK, doesn't come through to nurture each other. This is often when their relationship begins to die a slow death that can take many years.

If you love someone or something, nurture it. That means, at least once during the day, give the object of your attention or the person of your heart your full love. Even if just for a little while, listen to what they are saying. During this time, you are putting the little self aside.

The little self comes forward to meet the problems of the day, but put it aside to take time to just listen, love someone, and put your full attention on them, face-to-face. It's directly looking at the person you love, even after you are married. This is when the nurturing occurs and when the relationship is strengthened.

A good teacher makes sure the person understands what he's trying to say, whether he's communicating the spiritual principles of ECK or whatever. The best way to do this is to stop talking and ask, Do you understand what I'm saying?

15
For the ECK Arahata

These initiate meetings have a specific purpose. They give direction to you who are becoming Coworkers with God. How do you go about it? How do you serve under the direction of ECK in present society, working with me and those I designate as leaders?

Teaching Techniques

This is the Year of the Arahata. New people who approach ECKANKAR will need an Arahata, a teacher of ECK. There's a teaching form I unintentionally used on the phone the other day. I had lost track of what I was saying, and so I asked the person on the other end, "Where was I?" He said, "You were talking about so-and-so."

This is what a teacher does. A good teacher makes sure the person understands what he's trying to say, whether he's communicating the spiritual principles of ECK or whatever. The best way to do this is to stop talking and ask, Do you understand what I'm saying? When the answer is yes, you then say, "OK, what did I say?" and they'll tell you in their own understanding.

A teacher who does this well provokes a real discussion in a class. He can ask, "And do you agree? Is this what you see?" He's telling the students to take the unit of spiritual information and see beyond it. Maybe someone will tell him, "It's very good philosophy, but when I try it at home it doesn't work." When a problem surfaces, it can be addressed. This creates a hitch in the flow of conversation—which is good.

Life is a series of these hitches from beginning to end. That's what makes it so interesting. During a time of spiritual healing a whole bunch of hitches may come forward in your life. It's an opportunity. Hitches that come up in teaching are also an opportunity— first, to make sure you keep on track.

New people like to take the Arahata off on side trips. They talk about the other groups they've been in. If you're in college, why would you want to go back and chew over grade school? These people are afraid when they're new to a path, and they go back to where they feel comfortable.

Procrastination Hides Fear

When a person procrastinates, it's because he is afraid. This is very important for the Arahata to understand, especially when people begin procrastinating about something as spiritually vital as the Spiritual Exercises of ECK. Actually, these individuals are afraid something might happen.

They want something to happen but they wonder, If I try a Soul Travel exercise and it works, will I be up to it? They also know that after such an experience they would be forever different. And they would rather not be different. So they put off the spiritual exercises.

When people tell me they're not having any luck with the spiritual exercises, I ask them how often they're doing them. Usually they respond, "I try to get to them, but there's so much going on right now." If a person is not finding at least five minutes a day—let alone twenty or thirty—probably he is afraid of something.

Arahatas can ask, "What are you afraid of in the spiritual exercises? Are you afraid of the Light when It comes? Are you afraid of the Sound? Are you afraid of Soul Travel? Have you ever thought about why you might be afraid?" A person can take this into contemplation once he recognizes there is a fear.

People are afraid to find themselves in the other worlds. But once they get there, they often feel at home there. They feel they are at the peak of their spiritual development and they don't want to go back into the human consciousness. Their perceptions are clearer and higher than anything they have ever remembered. Yet as soon as they think of the human body, they come back into it; but they are never again the same.

From Dry Doctrine to Stories

We are becoming a teaching order based on stories to bring across the spiritual principles of ECK. This is the approach we'll need to meet the new generation of truth seekers coming to ECK who want to know how to reach the Light and Sound of God.

Use *The Book of ECK Parables* as a supplemental text in your Satsang classes. It will give you ideas of how to tie stories of your experiences to the ECK lesson. You'll learn how to do this.

In ECK today we don't put so much attention on the doctrinal aspects of ECK. That style meant you read paragraph one, asked for comments, then read paragraph two. Being in a class like that would be like listening to a very dry sermon. Instead we go through the discourse and use stories to illustrate the spiritual point being made in the different lessons.

The attention in religions used to be on where you went when life was over. Now there is a different emphasis. Today people are more interested in the spiritual life, how you make it work down here on earth.

Stories stick with the listener. People used to come away from an ECK talk feeling good about the philosophy, but they couldn't remember a word that was said. Now that stories are being used to illustrate the principles of ECK, they remember.

Encountering Inner Tests

If you have any questions, I'll try to answer them.

Q: Is the possibility of failing a test one reason that a person might be afraid to get out of his body?

HK: In school, I never liked tests, so I can understand that. But on the inner planes? I never actually considered the question of a test when I went into the other worlds. I just wanted to see what was there. My sense of curiosity was stronger than my sense of fear.

When the tests came, I didn't realize they were tests—no more than I realized the spiritual tests when they came out here. Usually when a test comes, you are not afraid of it because you don't know it's happening. It's the same on the inner planes.

Difference between Light and Sound

Q: Which is more important, the Light or the Sound?

HK: *The Spiritual Notebook* generally says that the Light comes first, then the Sound. In *The Shariyat* it says that everything comes out of the Sound. You get what you need at any particular time.

We tend to experience what we feel more comfortable with. Both Light and Sound are essential. The Light shows the pitfalls, and the Sound carries you home on the road to God. Generally, the Light is thought of as the first phase of coming into contact with the ECK works. It's not true, though, to say that the Light has to do with the lower worlds and the Sound with the higher. Both the Light and Sound operate through all the different worlds.

Some of us, because of our past experiences, need or want the knowledge of God at a particular time. This knowledge comes through the Light. Others are working between knowledge and wisdom. The wisdom is handled more directly through the Sound.

The Light is thus for people who are working with the knowledge of ECK, and the Sound for those who are working between the knowledge and the wisdom of ECK. You'll find at different times in your life that the emphasis will be on either the Light or the Sound. It depends upon what you need at that time.

You can chant HU quietly to yourself when you're faced with a problem or a person that's causing you trouble. Chant HU with love.

16
A New Level of Awareness

We will be expanding the creative arts at seminars as time goes on, as we find music that is appropriate to the highest spiritual teaching. Out of popular, rock, folk, country, and classical music, many people would pick classical as the most spiritual. It's not necessarily true. Levels exist in every category of music: there are the best, and there are the rest.

I like music that shows the lightness and happiness of Soul, and the different uplifting things that Soul faces every day. We'll continue to evolve the music of ECK so that it will touch all styles of music. Soul is happy; we'll have something happy and uplifting and enjoyable.

The Voids between Planes

Different voids occur between levels or divisions of the spiritual planes. The ECK teachings speak about one in particular, the one between the top of the Mental Plane and the Soul Plane. Yet each plane has a void between it and the next level. But also within the Second Plane there are a series of levels, or initiations, which also have their minor voids.

We're used to making an effort at climbing the mountain of God. We do the spiritual exercises, and we try to remember what happens on the inner planes. We try to remember our dreams. In short, we do everything we can. But in the void between one division and the next, it's as if an inversion takes place. The laws change.

When the individual reaches one of these voids, it feels as if he has come to an end, has stagnated. His spiritual word doesn't work; he may feel like his life is racing down on a roller coaster.

Moving Past Comfort Zones

When you get familiar with an area, it becomes your comfort zone. As you are ready to leave the comfort zone and go to the next level, you reach the void. In the void, nothing will happen for weeks, months, sometimes years. That's when you may say, "I want to get out of ECK. It doesn't work."

Moving too fast through the void, however, can be much worse than being in it. All of a sudden you're in the next division of spiritual unfoldment. The experiences are so different that you feel disoriented and upset. So you retreat back into the comfort zone.

Soul goes back to the previous level as quickly as It can, looking for an area It recognizes. Even though It no longer is having any experiences there, at least It isn't threatened. But then It becomes comfortable. That's when the individual begins to complain about the lack of experience.

This happens when a person is too afraid to go forward and just trust in the Mahanta, to go beyond the void into a new area.

How the Laws Reverse

When you pass through the void and reach a new area, you have to establish a new comfort zone. Establishing this new comfort zone can be an unsettling experience because the laws are all different. They change. I would like to explain it like this: If I were doing a spiritual exercise a certain way before, I would now reverse it in some manner, and then it would work. But it won't, because spiritual law doesn't just simply reverse as you get to a new level.

The laws change texture and do more than a flip-flop. They take on several dimensions at the same time which you know nothing about. This is a shock to Soul. When It comes into this kind of environment, It acts the same as a muscle does if it receives an electrical charge. It contracts. And Soul goes flying back to where It came from.

As Soul moves up the ladder again, It begins to have experiences similar to those It had before. The person is happy again. But he never realizes the experiences are very similar to the ones he's had before. And he will settle for these because he's afraid to go on.

The question is, How do you know whether you've entered the void? How do you know whether you're moving forward or going backward? Usually when you go ahead, the conditions are so different you don't know anything there. But if you've retreated, the experiences are very similar to what you've been used to. They may be more glorious, and therefore you are almost tricked into believing you are on the next level. But they are of the same nature.

Fasting in Times of Trouble

If the void were just an inner situation, you wouldn't have to worry about it. But it affects your work, health, and family. It shows up in outer problems. Somehow you've got to work through it.

When I'd run into a situation where other people appeared to be impossible to live with—it would've been easy to say, "That person has the problem," and go work somewhere else. But I'd try to work through the problem, if it was at all possible. I would go to extremes to work through it. If I couldn't work it out, I'd change the condition.

When it became more uncomfortable to live with the situation than to fast—when I felt backed into a corner—I would fast. You know the feeling—when you think you just can't take one more day. I used to do a partial fast to get through these periods. That means a fruit fast, one meal a day, or a mental fast. I always ate enough to carry on with my duties at work, but I'd put my attention on the Mahanta and chant HU. Under really severe conditions I would do this mental fasting every other day.

Spirit almost drives you through the void if you have the self-discipline to keep going. Spirit gives you the tools to fend for yourself.

Be careful when you do the different fasts. If you have a blood-sugar problem, it's not a good idea to go on a total fast. Today I wouldn't be able to do many of these fasts; my health doesn't allow it. You'll become irritable and tired and cause yourself more problems. You have to use a little common sense when you do these things.

Out of the Void

Usually you can pull yourself through the void with the Spiritual Exercises of ECK. Fasting goes hand in hand with the spiritual exercises. When you're doing a mental fast, you're really doing a spiritual exercise.

You can chant HU quietly to yourself when you're faced with a problem or a person that's causing you trouble. Chant HU with love.

The ECK discourses can help you understand the many different ways you are working as Soul, both here and in the other worlds. Once the Light and Sound melt the walls between the planes, you begin to see yourself working on all levels of existence at the same time.

I would like to thank you for the love and the service you are giving to the Mahanta, the ECK, and the SUGMAD.

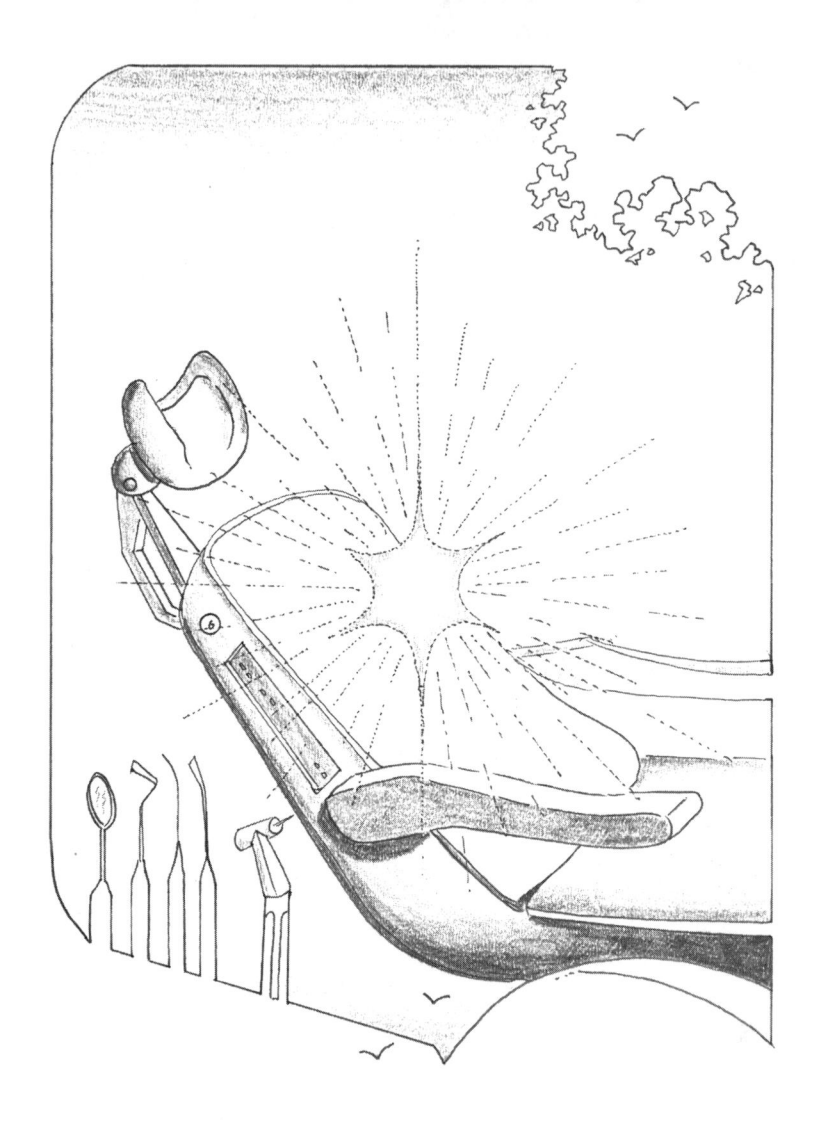

An Arahata is anyone who is teaching people about ECK when they ask, "What is ECK?" This doesn't always happen in a classroom. These questions may come at work, or even from your doctor or dentist.

17
The Law of Gratitude

This is the Year of the Arahata. Often when we think of being an Arahata, it's in a Satsang class. But an Arahata is anyone who is teaching people about ECK when they ask, "What is ECK?" This doesn't always happen in a classroom. These questions may come at work, or even from your doctor or dentist.

I was at the dentist getting my teeth cleaned about a month ago. He asked me what I did for a living. It doesn't really work to say, "My job description is Mahanta, Living ECK Master." So I said, "I edit some things sometimes," being really general. He probed further, "What do you edit?" This was taking place while I had my mouth wide open; I didn't want to talk, I just wanted to get the visit over with. But he prolonged it.

"I free-lance," I said. "Do you ever do books? What kind of books?" he asked. Gradually he edged it out of me that I work on ECK books. Next he asked, "Do you only edit?" "Sometimes I write," I said. And we had to go through the whole series of questions again.

"What Exactly Is ECK?"

Somebody gave my chiropractor some ECK books, and his staff got interested. He has about ten people working for him, scattered throughout his upstairs and downstairs office. At one of their morning briefings they discussed ECK before the patients arrived. That morning I went in for my adjustment. I got special treatment. "What exactly is ECK?" they wanted to know. Of course, they asked when the waiting room was full of patients.

As I explain ECK in these situations I'm acting as an Arahata. Sometimes it's not appropriate to explain ECKANKAR because of where you are at that moment: You have to be discreet and talk around the subject. But if a person really wants to know, if he sees something special in you, he will persist. He'll hound you for information.

Awareness of Life

Difficulties of health and other problems are part of going into the higher states of consciousness. Changes occur at every level of initiation. But the further you go, the more aware you become of these changes. So in a way, as your joy becomes greater, so does your capacity to recognize sorrow.

In ECK we're looking for higher states of consciousness. We're looking for greater awareness. Yet what is greater than the awareness of life in all its aspects? And how can you recognize these aspects unless you experience them?

I wish all experiences were pleasant, but they're not. This is how the SUGMAD has set up the lower worlds—for us to learn whatever we need to know.

Gifts of Grace

There's a difference between being a Co-worker with the Mahanta and a Co-worker with the SUGMAD. A Co-worker with the Mahanta is the initiate who is in training to become a Co-worker with God. A Co-worker with God knows his place in the spiritual hierarchy—what he must do, how he must blend in with the energies around him, how he must employ the Law of Economy to make the best of every situation. In other words, a Co-worker with God is living and working with the Law of Gratitude.

Gratitude is the attitude that allows us to be open to the gifts of the ECK and to continue receiving these gifts. But more importantly, it allows us to appreciate what we have right now—not what we had in the past or what we hope to have in the future, but what we have in our lives right now.

Gratitude allows us to recognize that what we have is exactly what we need for our spiritual unfoldment. What we have right now reflects our spiritual state of consciousness.

An Understanding of Mind Scans

Part of the growing awareness you are entitled to is an understanding of mind scans. These are done by people who are psychic busybodies, who are curious about your dealings because they feel they have a right to know what you do and who you are.

You can recognize mind scans by a headache that comes on suddenly. It's very localized, sometimes in the right temple, sometimes in the left temple, or sometimes in the back of the head. You may also perceive it as a band across the eyes that draws your eyes down. Generally it means that somebody is curious about something you're doing and he wants to make that information his own.

As we move into the twenty-first century, this kind of intrusion will be more common. It's generally done by one individual to another individual rather than by government propaganda. This is one-to-one combat, where a psychic thief is stealing something from you which he has no right to take.

When you get this headache, first you have to recognize there is such a thing as a mind scan. You might suddenly realize you are the victim of a mind scan but not instantly know the source of the scan. You have to trail it back. And as you trail it back to the source to find out who is doing this to you, you have to open yourself to the ECK. This means increasing your awareness of the people around you and of even yourself. Begin by taking inventory. Ask, What do I have that someone else considers important enough to steal through mental thievery? When you know yourself better, you can track back quicker.

Keeping Clear

Once you find out who the person is, it's best to begin gradually moving away from that individual. They don't understand something about spiritual law. While the person who is using the mind scan is often not consciously aware of it, he may be conscious of feeling jealousy or anger, or even hating you. This kind of overt behavior against you is a sign.

The mind scan is the unconscious taking of information. If you can catch it quickly, find out what is causing the headache, then figure out who hates you, is angry with you, or is jealous of you, you can gradually separate yourself from that person. That person is not doing you any good.

Long-Term Effects of Mind Scans

The short-term effects of a mind scan are only a headache. Long-term it can begin draining your health. Like a psychic attack over a long period of time, mind scans may cause a person's health to begin to fail.

Remember that no one can do a mind scan on you or give you a psychic attack unless you've allowed it. I'm putting the responsibility back on you. It's too easy to say, "I found out who's doing the mind scan. Villain, thief!" We forget that the person could never have done it if we hadn't opened the door to that individual.

How do we open the door? By keeping company with someone who hates us, who is angry with us, who is jealous or wishes to harm us in any way. We do this to keep up social appearances. We don't want to hurt their feelings. Or we fear—catch the word *fear*—that it will cause more problems if we turn our back on them.

When a mind scan occurs, the individual who is doing this has the unconscious ability, working through the Kal Niranjan, to give an autohypnotic suggestion: You will tell all. So when you meet that person, all of a sudden you find yourself talking about very personal, private matters—things you really didn't want to talk about. Later you might wonder, Why did I do that?

People who use mind scans also know, instinctively if not consciously, how to use the information against us which they have stolen from us. Often this can cause us a run of what we call bad luck, things going wrong.

I'm talking about something that's very subtle, but very real. In ECK we're ahead of the world in understanding this. As we approach the twenty-first century and the human race moves from the Astral to the Causal consciousness, this is going to become more of a problem. Long-term it can affect our health and our happy state of mind.

Soul is a happy being. This is the state we'd like to be in. We want to be happy, but we're not happy when we have headaches.

Law of Silence

When things go wrong, it's not because of the mind scan or the person using it. It's usually because we have not mastered the Law of Silence. People who talk to others about things they don't need to are empty in a way. The Law of Silence, if used, allows you to live within the Law of Grace, or the Law of Gratitude. These all tie together.

This information is very subtle. Each of your experiences is different. But those of you who have had experiences with mind scans in the past will begin putting two and two together. You'll say, Oh, that's what that was. After a time you'll also recognize the effect it's been having on you. Perhaps it's one of the reasons for any unhappiness or poor fortune you may have been having.

ECK is the path of love. It exists to bring each of us to a greater state of love. As we become filled with love, we are then magnets of love. As such we become pure channels for the Mahanta, while we learn to become Co-workers with the SUGMAD.

As we become filled with love and learn to be instruments of divine love, we become more conscious. Our lives become happier.

As time goes on you, as initiates, are forming a worldwide community of those who love ECK.

18
The Evolving Shariyat

It's interesting to travel from one culture to another. At one time Africa, Holland, Singapore, or Switzerland were just names on a map for me; I wasn't sure where these places were. But as time goes on you, as initiates, are forming a worldwide community of those who love ECK.

It's often an eye-opening experience to meet others at seminars who have come from faraway places. In doing so, we get rid of some of our preconceived notions about life in another country. In many ways it's similar, and in many ways it's different. But among chelas the love for ECK is really the same no matter what country we live in.

Firsthand Experience

Having firsthand experience from travel can shape your life in a whole new direction. Up until that time, you made up your mind about a place based on information you had read or heard.

It's the same with Soul Travel. Others have gone before us to the inner worlds as we are going now, and there are those to come. But as the Soul Travelers who have gone on ahead of us report back what they found, it isn't always a full report. In many of the inner worlds, there are vast areas still to be explored. But their reports do two things—they give us the incentive to go there, and they tell us what to do once we get there.

In ECK, the ones that go before us report back on the different conditions they faced and what a traveler can do to protect himself to fully explore these inner lands. The Third Initiate goes in advance of the Second Initiate, and the Fourth Initiate goes in advance of the Third. Everything that each of you learns in the other worlds and in this world benefits anyone who comes after you.

The sum total of your experiences are gathered together and addressed, in some form or another, in the Shariyat-Ki-Sugmad. The Shariyat is expressed here through many different forms; the *Mystic World* and the Wisdom Note are all drawn from the evolving Shariyat.

The Inner Side of Writing

Last winter I spent a lot of time writing *Soul Travelers of the Far Country*. Writing a book is gratifying on one hand, but it is also frustrating. Few writers work quickly. Writing includes constant rephrasing, reediting, and rewriting before it says exactly what you want it to say without overstating your point.

When you write about something, you are actually becoming whatever you are writing about. You are reliving whatever happened. A famous writer wrote a major novel about a particularly sordid period of World War II. During the middle of his experience of writing this novel, he wound up in the hospital for major surgery. All kinds of misfortunes befell his family. He never realized that by writing about such a purely negative incident, he was opening himself up to this string of misfortunes.

He could have shaped and directed the book in a number of different ways, but he didn't. When I write, no matter what I touch on, I like to bring in the uplifting element which is there, the spiritual lesson.

Change Is a Natural Process

Life is not a stasis, or steady condition, where change is a foreign element. Life is change itself. The mind, which likes to run in patterns, finds this very difficult to accept. It tries to look at things today pretty much the same way it did yesterday.

We can imagine life as a series of peaks and valleys. It's a continually changing spiritual terrain. We go from the valley to the plain to the mountain, then back down to the valley. This goes on and on. The transition from one area to another is a natural process of life.

It's Not in a Book

The experiences I write about at best can only inspire you to have your own. When Paul Twitchell wrote *The Tiger's Fang,* people would compare their own experiences with his and come up lacking. I think it's a mistake to model yourself too much after what is written in a book, whether it's by me or Paul or anyone else. The experiences that occur on the inner planes are of such vast dimension that you simply cannot hope to put into words the true meaning of what happened there.

The stories we've been given of heaven in the traditional scriptures are archaic. They are outmoded. It's as if you went to modern Jerusalem expecting all the people to be riding donkeys and walking around in long robes and sandals, when really there are cars, televisions, and running water. Modern residents of Jerusalem would wonder about you.

People of earth have such an outmoded understanding of heaven that they have no interest in going there in the Soul body to see it while they are living here in the twentieth century. They don't have any interest in finding out what's there and how it can expand them spiritually in all dimensions of their life. The best way to see the real heaven is through the Spiritual Exercises of ECK.

Putting Your Heart into Life

Doing the spiritual exercises is not like flipping through the weekly *TV Guide*. You can't approach them with the idle curiosity you use to browse through weekly TV listings—where you know what's available so you don't look very hard. With the spiritual exercises, you have to have more than idle curiosity. You have to put your heart into what you are doing.

When you learn this with the spiritual exercises, you'll begin to apply it to everything you do in life—your profession, your relationships, everything. We must put our heart and complete being into everything we do. To the extent we can do this, we are living in Soul consciousness. We are operating as the spiritual element, the Godlike awareness in its beginning stages.

But we have to begin somewhere, so we begin where we are today. We become more aware of who and what we are. We take care that whatever we do is the best we can possibly do under present conditions.

Deadlines

As an example, I have been working on a revision of *The Book of Spiritual Instructions for ECK Satsang Classes*. The new version is called the *ECK Arahata Book*. I asked the production staff at the ECK Office the latest possible date I could submit the new manuscript so that it would be ready for the ECK Worldwide Seminar. They gave me a date, and I set a week earlier than that for my own deadline.

That's how I work with deadlines, because something always comes up. If I plan to finish something at the last minute, I can always count on unexpected phone calls saying my help is needed in another area. If I set my deadline sooner than needed, it allows for the computer to break down or the printer to run out of toner at the eleventh hour, which they will do if they have a choice.

Illustrating Truth

A small manual such as the *ECK Arahata Book* cannot make anyone an expert teacher. What the book can do is give you a look at what the spiritual values are that relate to being an Arahata. It shows how to take the proper direction when giving the message to those who want to know more about truth as we know it on the path of ECKANKAR.

Writings like this may have the highest truth in the world, but if a book doesn't illustrate the different ways this truth may be expressed, it hasn't done its job. The truth may be the highest, yet if it doesn't relate to us personally in a way we can understand, the truth is lost.

Truth, after all, cannot be found in a book. It has to be found within yourself.

HU is spiritual food for all. The word *HU* has so much to offer the world today. We would be spiritually remiss if we tried to keep the singing of HU to ourselves.

19
Opening the Loving Heart

HU is spiritual food for all. The word *HU* has so much to offer the world today. We would be spiritually remiss if we tried to keep the singing of HU to ourselves. In the past we have opened HU Chants only to members of ECKANKAR; by creating the ECK Worship Service, we are taking another step into the world to broaden the scope of the ECK message.

A person who is overtaken by his own ego might say, "Let's keep ECKANKAR a closed teaching. It has always been given to just a select few, like myself. Let's not expand out into the world. Otherwise people out there will dirty the holy works of ECK." This attitude comes from a tendency to think that what we understand of the ECK teachings is the only important element there is.

It's hard to dirty the works of ECK, because ECK is life. Whatever is done in the name of ECK by a person is only a reflection of that person's consciousness. If it's a dirty consciousness, this person will pollute life. There's nothing to be done except give him time, more time to learn the lessons in the lower worlds.

Recognizing Unfoldment

When I have difficulty presenting ECK to someone, it's often because of the individual's hard experiences. Unfoldment has taken place, but it's unrecognized unfoldment. Unresolved problems mean unrecognized unfoldment.

If the wall of unknowing is strong, it's actually a good indication that a great deal of unfoldment has gone on. But until the loving heart, the Golden Heart, is opened, the individual is not aware of the revelation or realization he has gained.

Spiritual Warmth

Four families connected with the ECK staff had similar experiences right before this seminar. It showed me that the spiritual warmth had almost been shut off in the initiates because of hard times they had recently experienced. At the tail end of winter, each family had the experience of their furnaces going out or their hot-water heaters blowing up.

The common element in these appliances is energy. The energy was not there to allow these appliances to work anymore. To me it showed that the energy of the chelas was way down.

The blockage builds up and has to pass off into a cleansing stream. It doesn't happen instantly. When it gets to be too much, countermeasures are taken on the inner planes. This brings more warmth back to what seemed a cold spiritual life, where the individual has been practically pulped by hard experiences so there isn't much spiritual joy left inside.

From the Higher Planes

On the inner planes, I was standing on a hill overlooking a great plain. Across this plain lay a mile-wide band of hundreds of railroad tracks. The people of this world had decided that the coldness of the climate needed help.

They filled the tracks with steam engines, lined up like cars on a freeway at rush hour. The trains began to move from west to east, and the steam put warmth into the air in a huge band, across the world from left to right.

As I looked further in another direction, I saw people harvesting hay. It had been a long rainy season, but none of the hay had spoiled; it had grown instead. When the rain stopped, every member of each family was working around the clock in the field, bringing in the hay. The families were confident that their efforts at harvest would not be interrupted by an untimely rainstorm.

From this experience and others, I fully expect that many of the efforts which have been made to bring new people to ECK will be realized after this seminar. Also, the spiritual atmosphere which had been chilled will be warming up.

When I look to the inner and see these things, I just accept them. It's not something being shown to me about the future; it's something already happening in the present.

A person standing above the worlds of time and space finds that the past and the future are all part of the present. Here in the lower worlds we think of the past as separate from the present and beyond our reach. We think of the future as separate too. But from the upper planes, everything is seen in perspective, as one. Each has as much reality as the other. The past and future are contained in the present.

Cleansing the Soul Body

Many of you, as you progress in ECK, are changing your food habits quite naturally. You find that eating a certain food makes you feel better, and not eating another food also makes you feel better. Sometimes though, just for the fun of it, you'll go back and eat large quantities of something you've avoided for a while.

It may taste good, but now you find you have a much more adverse reaction to this food than you ever did before. It's because of this: You have brought cleaner and better food into your body. As you upgrade your diet, you find you can't go back. You can't do what you did before.

It's the same with spiritual food. As you progress in ECK, you find you are getting the spiritual food, sometimes unconsciously. The Light and Sound is coming into you as spiritual nutrition. And if you try to go back to the mental passions you used before—a full fury, gossip, or any of these things—the repercussions are much quicker and stronger than at any time in the past.

With the spiritual nutrition of the Light and Sound coming into you through the Spiritual Exercises of ECK, the Soul body has become much more sensitive. Before, you were able to get away with a certain lack of discipline with the mental passions. But now life hits you much harder when you regress. It's simply because you're beyond where you used to be.

Sometimes this brings mixed feelings. You say, Maybe I was better off where I was. But going back to what you were before also means taking on less consciousness. Soul finds it very difficult to go backward in consciousness.

When Consciousness Fades

Some people, however, do go backward; and their consciousness gradually fades. They're not even aware that they're less aware. You may see it very clearly, but often you're not able to say anything. You just have to let people follow their own lack of understanding and have their own experiences. They've forgotten the help that ECK gave them, and their consciousness is dimmed so much that they aren't aware of the blessings of ECK. A curtain of many layers is pulled between the conscious and the unconscious knowing of Soul. These people actually start traveling down the ladder of survival.

This is part of the process of life. Very few people advance toward God-Realization in a smooth, steady line. Generally you move forward quite a ways, then you come to a new area of understanding and fall back a bit. But if you stay on the path of ECK, you usually don't fall back as far as you were before you started this run up the River of God.

Be Concerned with Your Life, Not Others

When you see others leave ECK for a time or for a lifetime, it shouldn't cause you any concern. It's the nature of life. The only person's spiritual life that you should be concerned about is your own. How is *your* life going? When you fall back a little, it's OK. And then move forward.

When the loving heart opens in you, it means you are seeing the Light and recognizing the Sound of the Mahanta as It is manifesting in each one of you.

We're going through some changes in the future. I'll be taking the path of ECK more into the public, to make it available to more and more people. This means changes in the way things are being done.

There are many who will be able to keep up. Some others will pick an arbitrary time in the past and throw their anchors down at that spot in the River of God. But they will find that as the River of God changes course, they will be left high and dry on a shore which was once the life-giving river.

Times to come are going to be spiritually exciting. Whenever the channel for the Light and Sound is opened more fully than it has been in the past, it is a time for spiritual growth for everyone who wishes to be a part of it. I invite those of you who wish to, to come along.

When the film ended, one of the new people asked, "Could we do a HU Chant?" Out of all the different questions that could have been asked, this newcomer reached right to the spiritual heart of the ECK program.

20
Spiritual Healings

In every age, the teachings of ECK are given in a somewhat different way. The spiritual needs are different at that particular time, different than they've been before or will be in the future. The spiritual program is always custom-fit for the individual.

A good way to present ECK is to find out what the spiritual needs of people are and then try to help these people in every way possible on their way back home to God.

Spiritual Heart of ECK

An ECKist gave a "Journey Home" presentation. About 80 percent of the people there were attending their first ECK event. When the film ended, the room was quiet for a few minutes. Then one of the new people asked, "Could we do a HU Chant?"

That person realized that the HU was the way to learn about the Light and Sound of God. It was interesting that out of all the different questions that could have been asked, this newcomer reached right to the spiritual heart of the ECK program.

ECK Healers

I've been meeting with ECKists in the health professions to establish a way for licensed health professionals in ECK to get together. They can find out from each other what they have learned in their area of the healing arts as an ECK initiate and how their service to people has changed since they've become ECKists.

It'll be helpful for the entire world to have a nucleus of ECKists discussing ways for people to understand the spiritual aspects of their sickness.

In the future we're going to be reaching more people. They're going to be people with questions about healing, for instance. They're going to wonder about miraculous healings—why aren't there more in ECKANKAR, if it really is a true spiritual path? You get the chance to tell them, "Yes, you may get a miraculous healing in ECK, but you may not."

A Different Kind of Weather Report

A weather announcer on the East Coast of the United States was looking at weather in the Midwest one day, specifically in Minnesota. On that particular day Minneapolis had a higher temperature than any of the cities around it. It was cooler everywhere else.

Joking about it, the weather forecaster said, "Maybe something is going on in Minneapolis that the rest of us don't know about."

The date was May 5, 1988, and initiation recommendations had just been sent out from the ECK Office. This is what caused the hotter temperatures in Minneapolis. It was duly noted by the East-Coast weatherman who did not understand that he was giving a spiritual report that particular day.

Some initiates don't realize the vast amount of work involved in administering to the needs of so many people. I work with Higher Initiates who have proven themselves generally responsible. (I say "generally" because these are the lower worlds; everyone is still learning on the path to God.) Asking these High Initiates for recommendations is one of the ways I check up on the initiation qualifications of an individual, to see if that person is ready for the next initiation.

Delegating some of my duties is necessary. Otherwise it would only be possible for me to have about a hundred initiates. The rest of the world could just forget about ever hearing the message of ECK. But we're trying to reach as many people as possible with the teachings of ECK. If there wasn't a network of Higher Initiates and initiates at home to speak with new people, the greater mission of ECK would not be possible.

What Caused It?

Sometimes you ask a person what's wrong. He tells you, and you say, "Well, what do you suppose caused it?" Right away he backs off. It never occurred to him that there might be a reason for his problem or illness. He believes it is fate or destiny, something he doesn't have to take responsibility for himself.

Until recent times, a large number of healings were of this nature, where the person did not have to take personal responsibility for his own health. He got sick, he went to the doctor, the doctor gave him some pills, he took them, and he got better. And if he didn't take them, he didn't get better. He'd go back to the doctor, and the doctor would try to figure out another way to heal him, even though both of them knew the patient wasn't taking the pills.

In the past, healing has been very unspiritual. All responsibility for illness was pushed off onto someone else. The patient never had to take responsibility for having created his own problem.

Accept the Physical

We begin to age the moment we're born. We do everything we can to be as healthy as we can, but sometimes it's just not possible. Then we have to learn how to live with our condition and ask, What spiritual lesson are we learning as we go through this?

Use whatever help is available to make your life as pain-free and happy as it can be. If a person is selling a line of cosmetics which make you feel better, then get them because they make you feel better. But do it knowingly. Realize that anything of physical construction will wear out.

Realize, also, that you're in this physical body for purely spiritual reasons. You're not here for physical immortality but for spiritual immortality, to learn what you can to make your way in the physical world more pleasant. You focus on what you can learn from the ECK and from living every day to make life happier for yourself. Then you can be more cheerful, and the people around you can be more happy.

But if they are not happy, it's not your fault. It's their own. You're doing your part, and they have to do their part.

Chased by Spirits

I got a letter from an initiate. She wrote at the bottom, "This story probably should be shared." And I agree.

She and her husband were very behind in their

bills. They had a stack that had come due for payment, but she didn't know how they would make the payments that month. She thought she would write her brother Joe and ask him to lend her the money to pay the bills. She didn't know whether this was the right action, so she decided to try the Shariyat technique.

The passage she opened to didn't seem to have anything to do with paying bills. Maybe this is too frivolous a question to ask of the Shariyat technique, she thought. Maybe she should be asking something more spiritual.

At this point in the letter, she mentioned that she'd been having a series of nightmares. In these bad dreams, devils or spirits were coming on the inner planes and pushing her off tall buildings. She didn't know what to do to get rid of these nightmares. Then she told me, "I have a drinking problem." She didn't realize that when she spoke of devils or spirits, the Inner Master was drawing a parallel between them and the spirits of alcohol.

The alcohol was causing her to have nightmares. When the spirits in her dream were trying to throw her off a high building, it meant the alcohol was trying to throw her off a high state of consciousness.

She had just finished writing the letter to her brother Joe, still debating whether or not to mail it, when she noticed she was out of stamps. On her way out, she stopped by her next-door neighbor's house. While they sat on the porch, drinking, the ECKist heard her phone ring. Let it go, she thought. But it rang twenty times. So she ran back to her house to answer it.

When she picked up the receiver, the person said, "Hello, Carrie?" The ECKist's name wasn't Carrie. "You have the wrong number," she said. As she hung up, she suddenly remembered a movie called *Carrie* about a woman who was possessed; the theme reminded her of her nightmares. That's when the message finally hit her.

"Of course," she said. "I'm drinking, and that's why I'm having this very hard time with Divine Spirit. The Master's trying to tell me something about my drinking." So she went into contemplation again and opened *The Shariyat*. This time it opened to a passage that said that the initiates of the Fifth Circle "shall not use alcohol." She began to laugh. This series of events had a deep message for her.

Later that day she went to buy a stamp at the post office. Money was very tight, and she had her letter to Joe to mail. As she came outside with the stamp, the wind blew it out of her hand and under a car. She couldn't get to it. "All right, Mahanta, I get the message," she said. The Master was saying, "Do not mail the letter to your brother Joe. It's a problem you got yourself into with your bills, and you have to get yourself out. You can't get help from brother Joe."

As she walked around the car, the stamp blew from under the car. She used the stamp on the letter she would write to me, so that those of you who needed to hear this story could hear it.

Talk, but Mostly Listen

As you have the occasion to listen to people who need help, you'll find that many of them want to tell you about something that happened to them. Listen to them; tell them what you can, but mostly listen.

It's been said that as we get older, we try to tell other people how to do things the way we have learned them. But the things we have learned may not work for another person. If someone asks, we can tell. But if they don't ask, maybe we should just listen. Even if our advice is very good, we cannot live another person's life.

Perhaps the greatest kindness I can do for you is to let you know about the principles of ECK. I can show you how the rules of ECK are administered through the Holy Spirit, but it's up to you to live your own life. It's better than if I try to live it for you, and it's better if you give this consideration to others as well.

Allow other people the freedom to live their own lives. If you do this, you will be living the highest possible life you can as a vehicle for ECK.

Part Three

Becoming a Co-worker

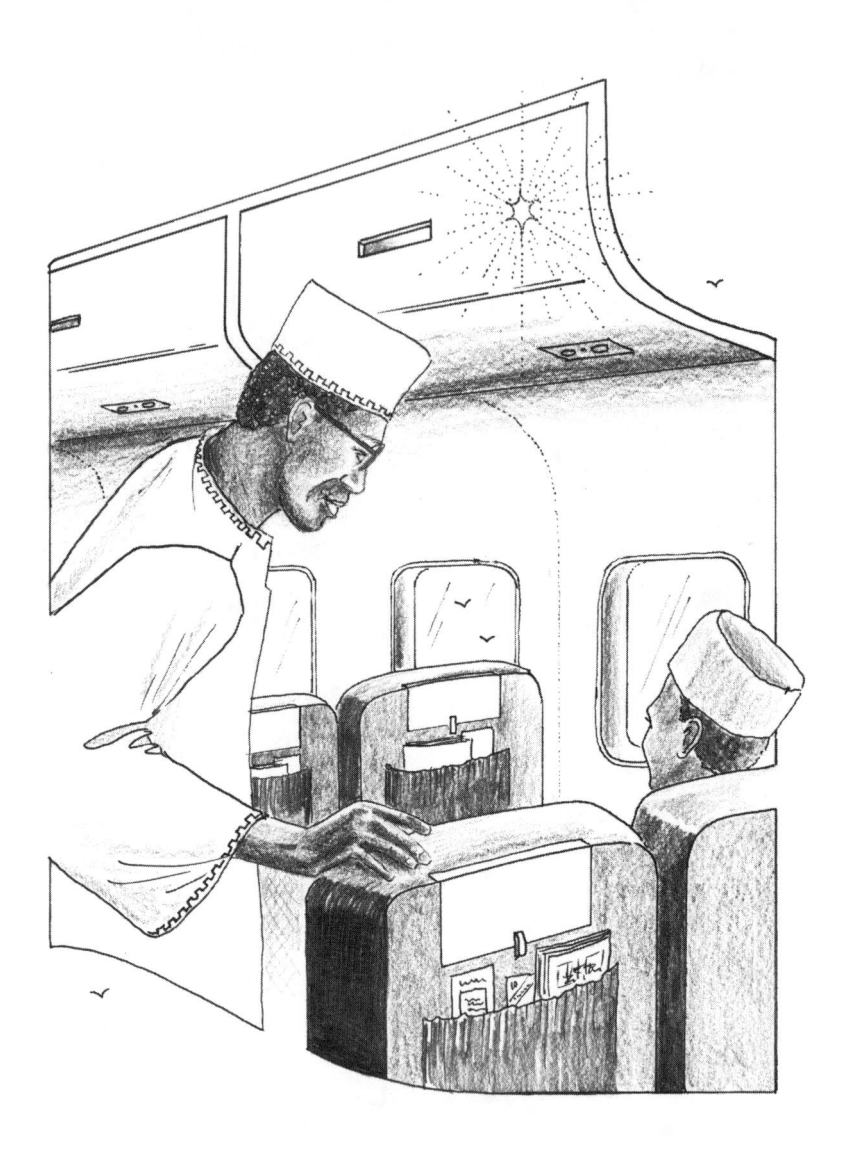

You'll often find in your travels that obstacles will come up, one after another, but in the end, if you're watching, you'll see how the Mahanta steps in to work something out for you.

21
A True Missionary for ECK

Usually on Friday nights, there's a wall that I feel when I come out to talk to the seminar audience. You've often faced one obstacle after another, and you're feeling lucky to have made it here. But last night the wall wasn't there.

Even though travel is still difficult, it shows that perhaps you are able to accommodate change and understand it better, perhaps not resist as much when things don't go according to plan. Because things hardly ever do.

Unexpected Gifts

One of the African initiates was traveling to an ECK seminar in Ghana. Travel is more difficult in Africa than in the U.S. This initiate got on a plane, and it was ready to taxi out onto the runway when the flight was suddenly canceled due to engine malfunction. The airport officials said that another plane would be along shortly.

The day passed and the night passed, and still no plane arrived. By the second day, the ECKist had been joined by two others traveling to the same seminar. By now they were a bit concerned about where to stay if they had another night's wait. The airport hotel was very expensive. The initiate passed the time reading *Journey of Soul*. He noted a passage about how going to an ECK seminar is like running an obstacle course.

That evening the initiates went to the hotel, and while they were there, they happened to speak with an airline official. They became quite friendly with him, talking and laughing; and everyone had a good time.

The next morning the replacement airplane came, but there were only six seats available for the sixty passengers. The ECKist who had been reading *Journey of Soul* told his friends, "Don't worry. In the end the Mahanta will come and work something out." But they didn't believe him.

It just happened that the airline official they had been talking with at the hotel was in charge of assigning the six seats. You can guess who got on the plane first—the ECKists. You'll often find in your travels that obstacles will come up, one after another, but in the end, if you're watching, you'll see how the Mahanta steps in to work something out for you.

A Different Kind of Missionary

In ECK we have a missionary effort. You and I are missionaries. We in ECK realize that when we go out as missionaries we also have something to learn. Perhaps the Christian missionaries believed they had all the answers, the only truth. This gave them an insensitivity toward the cultures they contacted for their missionary work. They often just pushed Christianity on others. They felt they had the right message and that it gave them the right to step on anyone they wanted to.

I hope that as you go out as missionaries for ECK you realize that in every meeting with a person who doesn't know about ECKANKAR, you have as much to learn as the other person does. In other words, it's a two-way street. As you give the message of the Light and Sound of God, there's an equal amount for you to learn.

If there isn't, then you are walking the old road of the Christian missionary. You would be overlooking the value of the present incarnation; you would be assuming you have all the answers already. When someone thinks that, he wonders why he has to bother with other people anyway. He overlooks the natural action of the ECK working to reach people when they are ready, not when we think they should be ready.

One Step Further

Many times as we are unfolding in ECK, we have to take things one step further. If we are careful about the little things, we find the big things take care of themselves. If we take care of our own lives, other things take care of themselves pretty well. If we take care of our own passions of the mind, we find we can live in this world without being stepped on by it.

People still trip us, perhaps, but there's a difference between stumbling and being sat on. Stumbling is just momentary. Being sat on can last for a long time.

In ECK we should be able to carry an experience one step further, to take one step further in our responsibility in a situation. When we do this, we are able to overcome many of the problems that come to people following paths where less awareness is required of them.

Turkey Potpie

To illustrate this in a very humble way, at home we have to be careful about lunch. When there's a large amount of work going through our office, my wife sometimes will call in a take-out order for food. We prefer to make our own, but sometimes there's not enough time. On this particular Monday, my wife called in an order for two turkey potpies.

We're careful with the people who take orders on the phone because they can overlook the obvious. We're used to little things going wrong, and we've gotten some funny orders in the past. This Monday my wife was being extra careful when she asked, "Do you have turkey potpie today?" The person said, "Yes, it's on the menu." My wife said, "Would you please go back to the kitchen and check?" It turned out they didn't have turkey potpie on Mondays, so we ordered something else. Her extra care saved me from having to wait for a half hour while something else was being prepared.

The next day we were still very busy, so we called back again. "Do you have turkey potpie today?" The counter person looked toward the kitchen, saw one potpie on the shelf, and assumed there were more. "Yes, we do," she said, and my wife ordered two.

When I went to pick them up, the counter person said, "The manager would like to talk with you." The manager was a woman with long blond hair and glasses. "I tried to call you back, but we wrote your phone number down wrong," she said. "We only have one turkey potpie. Since it was entirely my fault, I made you this turkey sandwich—it's free."

The counter person should have learned on day one to double-check, but she didn't. She wrote the phone number down wrong, which seemed a trivial detail since very seldom does the restaurant have to call a customer back on a take-out order. But it was important.

There are several lessons here. First, life teaches us to go past the first level of illusion. Even though it looks like turkey potpie is on the menu, it pays to check the kitchen. Go one step beyond what anyone else would do. Not just to save yourself grief, but to find out if there is more potential in the situation.

If you look one step further, it means you're working in consciousness which is one step greater, expanding one circle more than you had before. It means you're looking at things around you from more of a 360-degree viewpoint.

"There's Something Special about You"

One day I went into a corner grocery store in my neighborhood. It's run by a Korean man and his wife. The man has to stay up very late at night packaging his fruit and vegetables in plastic wrap; he has such a small store that he can't let the food go to waste. It's a difficult occupation.

He's never said much on the occasions I've been in the store, but I notice that he watches people. On this particular day, I was in a hurry, getting ready for the seminar. As I approached the counter and gave him money for the food I was buying, he said, "You belong to a special religion, don't you?" It caught me completely off guard.

Here was an individual who was asking about ECK, but he had only asked so much. I said, "Yes, I belong to ECKANKAR." He's still learning English and had a difficult time with the word *ECKANKAR*, so I spelled it for him and said it again very slowly.

I told him very basically that ECKANKAR teaches about Soul. "Soul is you and me," I said. "You and I have a body, but we are Soul. ECKANKAR is about Soul's experience with the Light and Sound of God. They're very real things; they're not imaginary." I figured I had done my half of the missionary work.

Then I asked him, "Do you belong to a religion?" He was a Methodist, he said. He had come from Seoul, South Korea, and he had belonged to several different Buddhist paths and also Shamanism. But now he was a Methodist. As I left, he said to me, "I've seen you and your wife come in here many times, and I knew that there was something special about you. I could tell from your eyes."

In the West, we are too often running and perhaps don't have the sensitivity that people in other parts of the world have. This man had a spiritual background, and what he noticed about me was important to him. I don't think I've ever been approached like that by someone raised in a Western culture.

In a Quiet Way

This is the kind of missionary work you will more and more find yourself a part of. We are making a conscious move out into the world with the teachings of ECK, more than ever before. It'll happen in a quiet way, not necessarily with the glitter and show that some people might feel is necessary for a new-age teaching. That's not what the teachings of ECK are about.

Thank you for being of service to those who have not yet gotten the spiritual strength in ECK that you have. Listen, and be available to anyone who would like to know more about the Light and Sound, Soul Travel, or dream travel.

Tell them what you can, but only give them as much as they ask for. Sometimes we tell people more than they ask for; we tell them what we think they should know. Maybe you could try telling them less than more.

This curtain is called lack of awareness, or ignorance. When it's gone, you have a much clearer view of your behavior and the effects of it.

22
The Curtain between Cause and Effect

I always look forward to the ECK Springtime Seminar. It's sometimes six months between the Worldwide and this seminar, but it's amazing to me how the winter flies by, even in Minneapolis.

It's been such a while since I've talked with you that I wonder if I will have enough to say. I wonder if I'll be able to say the right things that you need to hear, and which will be the best for you spiritually.

Sometimes someone backstage will ask me, "Don't you ever get nervous?" But giving a talk is very exciting for me. Listening to the ECK, working moment by moment as It changes the talk right out from under you, is a disconcerting thing. You can prepare all you want, but the talk may take a turn because of the needs of someone in the audience.

Priests in ECK

The media in Minneapolis has been very interested in us since we've started building the Temple of ECK. They've been interviewing one of our Fifth Initiates.

When they ask him if he's a priest, he says yes because the priesthood is a term they're familiar with. But there's a real difference between the priesthood in ECK and that of Christianity.

In the Catholic church, only a small segment of the people ever become part of the priesthood. Anyone who becomes a Fifth Initiate in ECK becomes a priest or priestess in ECK. This is a step toward Mastership. Each of you is actually preparing to become a Fifth Initiate, if you're not one already.

In ECK we have priests on different levels. The Higher Initiate who is able to listen to others in a spiritual way is an ECK Spiritual Aide. We also have the level of Initiators and the level of RESAs. These are just different levels of the priesthood in ECK.

Each person may go through these outer forms eventually. But they are just forms in this world to train one to be a Co-worker with God. It's a form that is familiar to the people we are trying to reach with the message of the Light and Sound.

As we put out a new level of outer teachings for the public, as we create ECK Worship Services for the public, it pushes other things, like our chela HU Chants, into the next level of secret teachings reserved for ECK initiates. It's a natural order. You are led to a door, and the door is opened when you are ready for it. We're broadening the base of ECKANKAR to reach the world, to go from being an introverted spiritual group to being an extroverted spiritual group. And we're doing it carefully.

The Issue of Abortion

On the issue of abortion, between pro-choice and pro-life, we find ourselves nicely positioned. Pro-choice is essentially where we're at—that a woman has the choice of whether or not to see the fetus to full term, where it becomes a child when it breathes the breath of life and Soul enters the body.

Pro-life is completely against abortion. I think that's because they don't understand the spiritual principle of when Soul enters the body. It's an old issue. To me, a fetus is a fetus. If organs such as the lungs and heart are not developed, the fetus cannot survive outside the mother's body. If a woman is pregnant and chooses not to have the child, she has plenty of time to get an abortion before all these organs are fully developed.

I feel it's an individual matter. If some kind of illness comes up where the doctors recommend an abortion in the seventh or eighth month, that should be the mother's choice, not the husband's or the government's or the pro-life group's. The woman is making a decision about her own life. This is how it should be.

Milarepa's Stone House

A Higher Initiate mentioned a Satsang class she attended. The class was discussing Milarepa. They talked about how Milarepa developed spiritual greatness through working with Marpa, his master. Marpa required him to build and rebuild a stone house at least three times. In the harshness of Tibet, I suppose three times is plenty.

When the H.I. left the Satsang, she didn't really feel too much rapport with Milarepa. What was the purpose of building a house three times, anyway?

The next day the woman got in the car to pick up her four-year-old daughter from preschool. She put in an ECK tape, and it was about the importance of initiate reports. When she got to the school, she found that her mother-in-law had already picked up the child, so the ECKist turned around and drove back home.

The unnecessary drive gave her the chance to hear about initiate reports. So when she got home, she decided to write a report. She turned on her computer and worked very carefully on this report for an hour and a half. It was the best report she'd ever written.

Most of you who work with computers know what happens when you do the best work you've ever done. The computer that usually never gives you a problem will suddenly lock up. It happened to her, and she had forgotten to save her work. The screen went completely blank.

As she sat there staring at the blank screen, the lesson of Milarepa suddenly came to mind. So she wrote a second report. Even though it didn't have the life and color of the first one, she learned something from it, and she got an insight into what the Satsang class had been all about.

Respect for Others

An ECK writer was working on a script in her cabin in the mountains. After she had carefully put together a section, she saved it onto a diskette and put the diskette away. I met with her in a restaurant about a month later. She was telling me about the work she had done, and I shared a little about my experience writing *Child in the Wilderness*.

"Only about 10 percent of the things I wanted to say went in the book," I told her. "There was more I couldn't say because the people involved are still living and I had to be careful of their feelings." She told me there were things in her script about her family, and she had been having nagging thoughts about what she had written. How would she feel if her daughter had tape-recorded her at her worst moments?

When she went back to work on the script, she found that all her diskettes were totally blank. The lesson came to her very strongly. Sometimes you're not able to write what you want, out of respect for other people who are still living. She got her lesson, but she lost a year's work. Not only that, but she had to give back the grant that had funded her work.

She learned something else: Her writing now had to move from the personal realm into a greater realm, which would make her a better storyteller. She looked at the dollar value of the grant and figured she had spent this much to learn about writing. As she understands the lesson, it will lift her to a higher level than she was at before.

As was the case with Milarepa, it can be crushing when the Master destroys the house we have so laboriously built. But this can happen because the Master cares only about the spiritual upliftment you are involved in, how to make you more suited to be a Co-worker with God.

How Initiate Reports Work Off Karma

Sometimes when this happens, it's as if you've run into a wall. You wonder what it is all about. Later you learn the lesson. It's a very direct method of removing the curtain between cause and effect in your own life. This curtain is called lack of awareness, or ignorance. When it's gone, you have a much clearer view of your behavior and the effects of it.

You can work out much of the karma you have through your initiate report. It will also remind you of things that have happened in the dream state, which is another place to work off karma and move forward on the path to God.

When the Inner Master works with you to teach patience, sometimes a creation of the ego must be destroyed once, twice, even three times before the light of Soul can come through. This is part of the purification you face.

Write the initiate reports by hand if you're afraid of the computer. Sometimes just a card is enough. It's for you more than for me.

Back Down the Mountain

Sometimes books like *Child in the Wilderness* are very difficult and painful for me to write because I'm trying to select those experiences that are spiritually helpful to you. They're not just told because they make a story. The events weave together into a point. The point of *Child in the Wilderness* is to show how the seeker goes up the mountain of God but does not remain there. He comes back down the other side and reenters everyday living.

When I read about the lives of saints who supposedly went up the mountain of God, I think maybe the mountain they're talking about was really just a foothill. It's hospitable enough on that foothill for a person to live in a cave away from the world. He can have other people serve him and take care of his needs. He can fritter away the rest of his life in meditation. The proof of a real God-Realized experience is: Does the person come down off the mountain and reenter life?

I've had many experiences with people who have. You will see these ECK Masters, because they are around. You see them when your curtain is raised, and it's raised only because of your love for God. And the love has to be so strong that you're willing to do anything to have this love of God.

Because you're so willing to do anything and everything for this love of God, you find some of the things you do aren't necessary and that you were following a delusion of the Kal. And so the spiritual experience is having to separate the real experience from the things that just helped incite the experience. It's very difficult.

What Is True Revelation?

True revelation is lived. It's putting the revelation into action that counts: when you go back into life and understand it from this new viewpoint. And believe me, it feels like you start at the very bottom.

You may have the greatest consciousness in the world, but it can seem like a curse when you don't fit anywhere. You don't fit with people who shared your beliefs before. Your friends are often ashamed of you, and you're completely alone. You have to reconstruct your world from little pieces, like Milarepa's stone house. Stone by stone, you put your new world together.

I had to learn certain lessons when I came back. I had to find a balance between a total disregard for the social consciousness and the God-Realized state. The social consciousness is necessary to maintain order in a society. Without it, you'd find out how very unspiritual people really are; this would be a barbaric society with little room for spiritual growth.

If you read *Child in the Wilderness,* I hope that somewhere in it you develop more compassion and understanding for people who think they have had a God-Realized experience but haven't. And compassion for those who may have had the experience but haven't put it into practice because they're still trying to put the pieces of their lives together.

Child in the Wilderness is an important book in spiritual literature. It shows what to expect from a God-Realized experience and how to work your way back into everyday living. May you see in it a guideline for your own mastership.

Every Soul's destiny is spiritual liberation; it's for every Soul. One Soul is not greater or less than another Soul.

23
Soul Equals Soul

A unity is coming about in Europe, Africa, and the Far East because of the influence of ECK. People in Europe are coming together, perhaps for the first time. In the past, the Romans and other people attempted to unite Europe by conquest, but they have all come to nothing. This time the people of Europe are coming together because they want to, not because someone is trying to rule them.

Learning to Work Together

We are living in an unprecedented period of history. To succeed, people will have to learn to work together. And ECKists have something to learn from the European countries in how to work together peacefully, agreeably, and eventually lovingly.

The history of mankind has been blackened by wars. What are wars but the vanity of one group of people taking control and trying to impose conditions on another group? The stakes are personal and national freedom, and when they're great enough, the oppressed fight off the oppressor. This is war.

If humanity has learned anything, it should be that

hate and anger require a big price. Perhaps mankind moves forward during war, but it will move faster toward a greater consciousness if people learn to work in harmony with their next-door neighbors.

A Historical Moment

At this point the Temple of ECK is being manifested on the physical plane. We have several other ECK Temples that already exist on the physical, but most are on a supraphysical level, which means that not just anyone can get there.

This temple in Minnesota is available to people everywhere. It will be a temple that anyone can walk into. It is a matrix of spiritual power on earth for the physical universe and the Seat of Power for ECKANKAR.

Sometimes we don't recognize the importance of a historical moment because it's too close. Even as the unity of the European communities is manifesting before our eyes, the spiritual upliftment of the human race is occurring. You'd expect everyone to say, "What a joyful time!" Not so surprisingly some people say, "But it means giving up the old ways."

Giving Up What You Outgrow

It doesn't mean giving up all the old ways, just the old ways that are outgrown. There is always a transition in change from the past to the present.

Hardly ever do we jump into the future without taking some things from the past with us. But we take the good and necessary things, and we leave the baggage behind. The baggage is that which has caused us nothing but storage problems and heartache. It's that which we carry even though we no longer need it.

Soul Equals Soul

Our goal is spiritual freedom. It's a goal which is available to every Soul, not just to you and me. Too often in the past we have been selfish in our desire for spiritual freedom. We thought of it like this: *I want to be spiritually free; I want to do as I please.* Meaning, *I want to do as I please no matter where I am or with whom I walk.* It meant wanting spiritual freedom without regard to another's freedom.

The problem comes when one Soul says, "You are less than I am." An individual who says that has plans for another person's life: You will work for me, and you will like it. But Soul equals Soul. Every Soul's destiny is spiritual liberation; it's for every Soul. One Soul is not greater or less than another Soul.

Moving ECKANKAR to the Next Step

In ECK we have had a narrow view of liberation since our founding. We wanted freedom for ourselves without ever thinking that this freedom must also be available to others. This is why every time I move ECKANKAR around a corner to get it back on track, there is some opposition.

For example, some people don't like the way I describe Paul Twitchell. They have an idea of how Paul was, even though they never met him physically and seldom on the inner planes. The human consciousness sees things as either right or wrong. And a person of a narrow human consciousness says, "That is right, this is wrong." A person like this cannot let things be, cannot obey the Law of Silence, but must convince others that they are wrong.

They create problems among people. We have our own little wars led by people who are full of anger.

When there is no love inside, there is room for something else. Nature will not have a vacuum, so the person is filled with the opposite of love.

In this next year the most difficult thing for us to do will be to learn how to be partners with life, or Coworkers with God.

Along with this comes the idea of people who wish to jump directly from the human consciousness to God-Realization. It never occurs to them, because they do not have the understanding, that this is not possible. You cannot go directly from the old to the brand new without any area of transition in between. There needs to be time to change.

And so at this point, it's time for the Temple of ECK to be built in Minnesota. I've written an article in the *Mystic World* (Fall 1989) in which I go into some detail to place it among the other Temples that already exist on the physical plane, but which are not accessible to most people.

The Temple of ECK

The Temple of ECK in Minnesota is a Temple of Golden Wisdom. It will become a center, both inwardly and outwardly, for spiritual teaching, for the dream teachings, and for Soul Travel. It will be the place from which the spiritual teachings of ECK reach out into the physical universe, especially to our own planet. This is a very important time in spiritual history.

The Temple stands for something. It stands for the possibility of humanity moving to a new level of consciousness. But this possibility needs you, the ECK initiate, to be an example of ECK for the world, to be an ambassador for ECK. To bring the teachings to people in a way they can understand.

For this reason we have put together in a unit called the ECK Worship Service, different ECK practices we have already used in the past. This includes reading of ECK scripture, singing the HU, and discussion of ECK principles. I'm calling them public worship services because I can't think of a better word that relates to the people in the world. It has to be a term they understand.

To most people, the ECK terms mean nothing. Some of these terms are very important to us—*ECK, SUGMAD, Mahanta.* But we change them off with *Holy Spirit, God, the spiritual leader,* or *a high state of consciousness* to explain the words that people in the world would not understand. If they can't understand, they won't get any truth from us.

There are initiates who say, in effect, "Let's exclude the people of the world from what we have learned as truth." They call themselves purists, but they are unable to distinguish between form and function. The ECK terms are only to express a spiritual principle. We say, "SUGMAD," and we refer to the principle that caused life. But God is God whether we call IT *SUGMAD* or not.

Are You Part of Life?

We have the Temple of ECK, and we have the ECK Worship Service. And we're going to grow into this because there is a unity of spiritual consciousness that is occurring on earth. We can either be part of and help this chapter of spiritual history, or we can excuse ourselves from life.

No matter which we choose, this spiritual chapter is still happening. The choice is always ours. Divine Spirit, or the ECK, is always manifesting change in greater and greater worlds. As we move with It, the old, useless things are left behind. They no longer belong. Not the old, necessary things; but the old, useless things are left behind.

The human race is moving into a higher state of awareness. It won't happen by itself. It needs help. As partners in life, you can help. And how do you help?

Many people who came into ECK at the beginning did so because they thought ECKANKAR was cut off from life. They said, "This is perfect. I don't like this life either, so I will join that organization."

Now we are moving into life where we belong, because we are the leaders in life. At this point you must look at your beliefs and ask yourself, Did I misunderstand ECKANKAR when I came in? Is it really a path for a recluse or a hermit? Or is it a path for a Co-worker or partner with God?

There's an ECKist here in Holland who told me about a custom. One of the neighborly functions is to go out on the frozen dikes in winter and drink cocoa. It forms a community of people who share friendship with each other.

I think being partners with the SUGMAD or with life means to go out on the ice and have cocoa with your neighbors.

If I have the point of view that my hotel room is holy ground because I am there, I will do whatever I can to leave it in as close to the same condition as I found it.

24
Your Life as Holy Ground

People outside of ECK wonder what ECK has to offer them. They hear we have a direct link with the Voice of God and they wonder, How does God speak to us? And if God speaks to me, what will the result be? How am I going to be better off for it?

The simple answer is, You'll have more peace of mind.

Life has plenty of ups, downs, and uncertainties because this is part of the purification that Soul goes through to become a Co-worker with God. But if you learn how to listen to the ECK, It can bring you peace of mind. You learn to sidestep the harshest attempts of life to bring you to your knees. You dodge the spears of life and come through the gauntlet pretty unscathed.

Are You an ECKist Too?

The ECK community is not only worldwide, but sometimes closer than we think.

An ECKist wanted a pendant with ECK on it. It had been on her mind for several seminars to get one, and finally she did. She lives in a small town in Canada.

Some friends of hers run a café; the wife is the cook. The ECKists have gone in there many times, but they've never mentioned ECKANKAR to their friends.

When the couple came back from the seminar, they went to the café for dinner. The ECKist was wearing her new pendant. Her friend, the cook, came out of the kitchen to chat and saw the ⊖, but she didn't say anything. The ECKist who was wearing it wondered, What do I say when she asks what it is?

Finally the cook said, "Are you an ECKist too?" Canadians are somewhat reserved. In California if one person had seen another with an ⊖ pendant, they would have immediately jumped up and hugged each other.

Sacred Routines

In ECKANKAR, we are going through many changes in a relatively short period—the establishment of the RESA program and the building of the ECK Temple. I'm aware that for a few the change is coming almost too fast. But most of you have adapted very well to it.

Most of us don't like change because our routine is something we've developed carefully. Routine includes such things as a favorite easy chair at home after a hard day's work or a favorite restaurant over the weekend. If you're used to going to a certain restaurant for Sunday dinner and your spouse suddenly wants to go somewhere else, there will probably be a reaction. Unless there's some really good benefit to making the change, you can expect resistance.

In spiritual unfoldment, too, we have developed our precious routines which give us peace of mind and stability. They shelter us from the outside world that we deal with every day. Your routine recharges your batteries. But sometimes there's a need to make a change for spiritual reasons.

Resistance to Change

Someone told me the story of an audio salesman who worked for his company. The salesman's name was Ed, and he had an idea for a revolutionary way to set up an audio sound system. The other salesmen gave it a lukewarm reception, but Ed went ahead with his idea for the benefit of the customers.

The result was a much better sound. Customers walking into the store could tell right away, and sales went up. The company launched a special advertising campaign that brought in even more customers. Even so, the older salesmen still resisted the change. They had their own ideas about how to set up the equipment, even though Ed's system worked better.

When people resist change, there will often be no logic to it. All the benefits in the world can be staring them in the face, but they resist anyway.

I point this out so you can check yourselves. When you feel resistance, ask yourself, How is my routine being threatened? Can I examine myself? Can I take it to the inner planes in contemplation to see if I really have a reason for resisting this change? Or am I holding myself back spiritually?

Remember that if you're holding yourself back spiritually, you're probably holding up several others. If you're on the path of ECK and you have resistance to change in ECK, you may be hurting the little band of people who look up to you. This is a great responsibility of being a chela in ECKANKAR. ECK is the path of change; you've got to expect this.

A Broader Perspective: The Goal of ECK

When change comes, ask yourself, Has the goal changed? Or have only the means of achieving the goal changed? The goal is always the same—for the individual to become a Co-worker with God. And in becoming a Co-worker with God, the goal is always to find others who are ready for the ECK teachings so they can also become Co-workers with God. That is the purpose of ECK.

We want spiritual freedom, but not simply for the self; it should not become an end in itself. We want spiritual freedom that takes the next step and gives service to God. This is the full measure. To be a Co-worker means to help each other.

Moving to the Causal Initiation

A number of you noticed the connection between the ground breaking for the Temple of ECK and the political upheaval in East Germany and the subsequent toppling of the Berlin Wall. Within a few days of the ground breaking, the impossible happened—the government of East Germany toppled. It even caught the newspeople in the West by surprise.

In talking to the Spiritual Council about this, I tried to tie together the spiritual thrust which is occurring right now. Humanity is on the borderline deciding if it wants to move forward to the Third Initiation or fall back into the Emotional Plane. We know what the emotional level of consciousness is. It has been responsible for so many of the wars that we have seen in centuries past. Humanity is now deciding whether or not to move to the next level of awareness.

When it has learned the same lesson often enough from every different angle, then it will be ready to leave the second level and move to the third. It will have to make that decision. It's not something I determine.

Even though the mass of humanity does not progress in even steps, there are enough leaders to carry the movement forward. What will be the outer manifestations as the leaders of this spiritual movement begin to act? You're seeing evidence of it already. The leaders are the people who are looking at the causes of man's effect on the earth. They're beginning to examine what has happened to the environment, how we have misused our natural resources, and other effects of mankind's ignorance and greed.

If the rest of humanity agrees to be responsible for their actions, responsible for our physical home of earth, that will be the surest sign that mankind is moving into the Causal Initiation. Because the Causal, or Third, Initiation looks at causes. In your individual life you become more aware of the forces that have brought you to your present station in life. In the world at large, it is exactly the same.

Science has brought us many benefits, but we are aware now that the consequences have revealed themselves at a much slower pace than the benefits. For example, during World War II the scientists developed radar. Now there are concerns about electromagnetic fields and their effect on health. Some are examining the effects of power lines running through a neighborhood. There are concerns about the greenhouse effect, the warming of the planet. People are starting to look at their responsibility in having made earth less habitable. A change will take place as the consciousness tries to keep earth as livable as possible.

Holy Ground

The consciousness of people today has reached a higher level. People are recognizing that wherever we live is the holy ground of God. It's not enough to say, We'll be here for just a short time; then we'll leave, so let's not worry about the problems we've caused polluting the streams and the lakes. It's not enough.

If I leave my hotel room a mess, I know it doesn't matter because the hotel maid will clean it. She's paid to do that. But if I have the point of view that my hotel room is holy ground because I am there, I will do whatever I can to leave it in as close to the same condition as I found it.

I want to make this connection for you about the importance of the Temple of ECK. Even now, before it's done, it has a presence. This feeling is also noticed by the workers who come there and know nothing about ECKANKAR. They're curious and ask, "What is this building?" They can feel it. There is something special about it.

When you come to visit the Temple of ECK, I think you'll feel the presence of this very special Wisdom Temple. It is now being built on earth for a very definite reason: To be available when mankind reaches the decision to move to the Causal Initiation.

Whether they are animal, child, or adult, something binds them all together. That is the love of God, or the love of ECK. This love is working every day in my life and in your life.

25
Expressions of Divine Love

Since we last met, the Berlin Wall has come down and the Iron Curtain is a bit more ragged than it was before. We can consider this not as a sign of peace on earth forever, but as a window to allow the message of ECK to get to people who haven't been able to get it openly before.

Earth is to help people become more spiritual beings. If there truly were peace on earth among mankind, there wouldn't be any reason to have earth. Earth isn't quite ready to stop being a classroom yet. If earth is still here, we can expect that people are still learning—and contending with the five passions of the mind.

Less Time but More Love

There's a family in Minnesota with a lot of children and pets. The mother wrote me that she sometimes envied single people because they could do as they pleased with their time. This mother spent her time taking kids to school and sporting events, and she wondered why there was so little left over for herself.

Then she read a book that counseled single people

on how to feel less lonely. She had noticed this loneliness in single people. The mother realized that her own life—with her husband, children, and pets—was so full she never had time to be lonely. With her decision to have a family, perhaps she gave up other things. But she realized that she had the greatest blessing—she had love in her life.

This is how it often is. We don't recognize our blessings. We always look across the fence and think, The food is better there; the grass is greener.

Feeding Insight

The family had a dog that didn't like dog food. It ate the cat food, and it ate human food. The children threw it carrots and other items they wanted to get rid of. To solve this problem, the family tried to interest the dog in all kinds of dog food. The dog didn't like any of them, but it would still eat cat food. The family finally had to put the cat's dish up on a shelf to keep the dog from eating the cat food.

One day the husband was doing his spiritual exercises, and because he did them he had an insight. He said to his wife, "Feed the dog from the cat's dish. Give it dog food in the cat's dish." And the dog loved it. He'd eat any of the ninety-nine brands of dog food he wouldn't touch before—if they were served in the cat's dish. And so often this is how we are too.

The Common Bond of Love

One day the cat cornered a squirrel in the sandbox out in the yard. The mother and young son ran out to rescue the squirrel, and the dog followed them. The mother grabbed the dog to keep it away from the cat, as the boy grabbed the squirrel. Then the mother yelled, "Let go of the squirrel; it may bite. Grab the cat." So the boy put the squirrel down, and it ran up a tree to safety. The mother was telling me that these things happen in her family every day.

She realizes, however, that all these little things are expressions of divine love. There is love between the mother and child; that's why she ran outside to help him rescue the squirrel. The dog came out because he loves the cat—and probably he loves mischief too.

A New Haircut

The dog and cat are good friends; they get along very well. But during summer the family decided to give the dog a haircut. The cat slept in the coolness of the basement all day. When the cat came back upstairs that evening, there was this strange-looking dog in the house. The cat avoided it for about a day or two. Then the cat realized, "Oh, it's just Sandy." And the cat went back to pestering the dog.

People are like this too. When things get hot, we like to disappear, especially if there's trouble around. People get rid of some hair, or some karma. The Mahanta gives Soul a haircut. After his experiences the ECKist comes back into the community of initiates, and they think he's a stranger. "He's different since his experience," they say. But after a little while, they realize That's no stranger, that's our old friend, and draw him in again.

The dog, cat, squirrel, child, and mother are all different. But whether they are animal, child, or adult, something binds them all together. That is the love of God, or the love of ECK. This love is working every day in my life and in your life, and in the lives of your friends and family and neighbors. This love is drawing you together. You need people, and they need you.

Often we act as if we are the only people on earth. We act as if we don't need anyone else, as if we are the only ones worthy of love. We are like selfish kings and queens, walking the earth, taking and taking and never giving back.

Natural Balance

A woman in Holland has two cats, a long-haired cat and a short-haired cat. When she gets busy and feels very empty, all of a sudden she hears the meow of the long-haired cat. This cat came to this world to give love. The short-haired cat came to take love. If she's feeling too much love, the woman gives it to the short-haired cat. If there isn't enough in her, the long-haired cat comes to give the woman love. Within this circle of herself and her two cats, we see divine love working.

Divine love works with you and your loved ones, but you need to stop and recognize it. You ask me, "How do I know if I have God's love working for me now?" My answer is the Spiritual Exercises of ECK. Do them. If you have no time for anything else, have time for them. Because as you do them, you will get a greater awareness of what you can do to make your life run better.

Shortages

We most often get upset when we are faced with a shortage—a shortage of time or money. Often the shortage is due to our own lack of planning. When we're short on time or money, we become short with the people around us. We become angry, ill-tempered.

We are saying, "I don't have time for you; I'm too busy."

When we tell others, "I'm too busy," we're really saying, "I'm too important." This is the ego speaking. It's saying we have no time for the Mahanta's love, for God's love. We are too busy to do the work of God. And the first work of God is to do the Spiritual Exercises of ECK. When we do them, we learn how to make our lives run better because we learn to plan better.

Money is no different than time—they're both commodities. We can plan our money just as we plan our time. But it depends on us to plan. Time is a temporal thing. When the worlds pass away, there will be no more time. Time is a resource to use well. Time, money, and everything else are gifts from the ECK to use well for our experience.

Letting Divine Spirit Work in Your Life

Left all to our own devices, our plans don't work as well as they could. But by doing the Spiritual Exercises of ECK, we open ourselves to the planning of the Holy Spirit. Then our so-called misfortunes and mistakes in life work out. They work out to help us in the best spiritual way possible.

As we go into the Year of the Vahana, we must first open ourselves to the spirit of love. Unless we have love, we won't have time to serve God.

Keep your face to the Mahanta, to the Inner Master. Keep your heart open. And keep your Spiritual Eye open to the source of divine love. If you are to be greater in life in any way, it's only because you know of the Spiritual Exercises of ECK. They can make you a greater spiritual being, and one day a Co-worker with God.

As mankind unfolds, man is going to have to learn to work with his neighbor. We're not looking for peace in this warring universe, but we are looking to learn how to work with each other. Unless we do, we cannot become Co-workers with God.

26
Partners with Life

I've been spending much of my time in the last few years writing about God-Realization, how important it is, and what it means. *Child in the Wilderness* gives my experience in this to put alongside *The Tiger's Fang*.

False Jumps

I find it odd that there are people who say, "I am in the human state of consciousness today, and tomorrow I'll be God-Realized." In one big jump.

But in making this jump to what they imagine God-Realization to be, they are making a false jump into a condition that is neither spiritual nor helpful to anyone. When they declare themselves to be God-Realized, either directly or by suggestion, they simply are looking to gather followers. To them, God-Realization equals having followers. They get so interested in this—at whatever cost to themselves or other people—that they forget about living life. They forget the purpose of living life.

So for a period of time, I'm going to put attention not on the state of God-Realization but on the process of life, on day-to-day living. Because God-Realization is not a state where one becomes self-serving. It's a state where one serves others.

Spiritual Growth Is a Process

So many ECK initiates have the feeling that nothing happens in between human consciousness and God Consciousness. They're impatient, for example, to get through the Second Initiation because they want the Third. This is also true of many Higher Initiates.

It seldom does anyone any good to get an initiation too early. Paul Twitchell gave early initiations in his day simply because he needed the vehicles to help him carry out his mission. But many of these people have left ECK.

When a human being gets something too fast and too easily, he finds it a treasure of almost no value. He becomes arrogant. And when someone becomes arrogant with something as spiritually powerful as the ECK teachings, they burn out. That's why so few of the ECK initiates who were given early initiations years ago have survived in ECKANKAR today.

When the trials come, they don't recognize them as trials. When the test of faith comes, they don't recognize it as a test of spiritual faith. They judge everything according to the human consciousness—it's either right or wrong. Not in the absolute sense of the ECK viewpoint, but as they see it. Something is wrong because they do not understand. And, of course, they do not accept the fact that they do not understand these things.

The human consciousness does not allow a poor opinion of itself. So when the individual is working from the human consciousness and he does not understand something, he figures it must be wrong. This creates a loop, like a kitten chasing its tail. It sees the tail, bites it, has pain, and complains. It's chasing something, but it happens to be itself. That's how the human consciousness and the mind work.

Unity of Consciousness

I see very good trends in Europe—the European Community and cooperation between separate units of Europe. These countries have been at each other's throats for centuries. Not because it's a problem in Europe, per se, but it's a problem of the human consciousness. In ECKANKAR we recognize reincarnation; we know that we have all been here fighting the wars against each other in the past.

If cooperation between these separate units of Europe can work, there may not have to be another major war among the people of these countries. Perhaps this unity will serve as a guide for ECK initiates, so that there can be a working together of Higher Initiates, not just between countries, but within a country. Once this happens, it will be proof that the consciousness of the ECK groups in Europe has reached a higher level of spirituality.

We know this is a warring universe. But as mankind unfolds, man is going to have to learn to work with his neighbor. We're not looking for peace in this warring universe, but we are looking to learn how to work with each other. Unless we do, we cannot become Co-workers with God.

Kind to Ourselves

One of the definitions of *Co-workers with God* is "partners with life." This means, first, that we must learn to be kind to ourselves as individuals.

This even applies to the Friday fast. There are three levels of fasting. If you have a health problem, I would not suggest the water fast at all. By doing without food, some people harm themselves spiritually more than if they ate something on Friday.

I did the water fast when I was younger, and my body could adjust to the shock. I would not be able to do it today because I'm older. I don't expect people to forget their common sense when it comes to the Friday fasts.

There are two other kinds of fasts that may fit you better. You can do a juice or partial food fast; or you can do a mental fast. The mental fast is done by keeping your attention on the Mahanta, the ECK, or the SUGMAD. In the spiritual sense, there really is no difference in the three. In a human sense we can differentiate between the three and end up calling them things like the Father, Son, and Holy Ghost. But that is the mind trying to make divisions and separations so that it can try to understand something that is really not within the scope of human understanding.

Life is a unity. There is a cohesiveness that binds life from one end to the other. This cohesiveness is love. If we have been defining love from the human consciousness, then the definition may need redefining. Divine love does not impose itself upon another person. It allows others to live, move, and have their being.

Agree to Disagree

Sometimes an ECKist comes to me and says, "I have inner guidance that tells me to do something the RESA has told me not to do." We have to understand that on earth neither the chela nor the RESA is absolutely correct. Within the spiritual administration, I have asked the RESA to be my representative in an area, to make the best decisions he or she possibly can. The RESA is not more or less sanctified or holy than anyone else.

Sometimes you may agree with the RESA, and other times you may not. If you cannot agree at all, just let the situation be. Step back. Our opinions tell us we are so right and the other person is so wrong. But what we are saying then is, "I, as Soul, am greater than that other person." If we had any understanding at all about the Ocean of Love and Mercy, we'd know that Soul equals Soul. Soul is not greater or less than another. Soul equals Soul.

When we remember this, we can have respect for another person. This respect begins with ourselves. First we must respect and love ourselves. Sometimes we are more willing to harm and criticize each other than to get along with each other, than to love each other. We may not always agree, but we can observe the Law of Silence. Or you can write to me. If there is really something to be done, I'll consider it.

Careful Changes

The higher you go spiritually, you are not often as free and able to make changes as quickly as you would like because of the spiritual harm you could do to someone else. When I see a problem between two initiates, I'll often let the situation run for a year or two. Not because I enjoy seeing people fight with each other, but because if changes were made right away, it could do immeasurable spiritual harm to others around them. Because of that condition, I am slow to make changes sometimes.

Each RESA area is like a country in the European Community. Each retains its individuality, its language, its uniqueness, but they find they have something in common. They find it more to their advantage to work together than apart. Spiritually, this is the purpose of the lower worlds, to learn to work together to become Co-workers with God. It's no mistake there are so many different languages in the world, different cultures. And understand that each culture means looking at things in a different way.

Unless we learn to work together, we cannot become Co-workers with God. We must somehow find a way to work with those we find it hardest to work with. We want spiritual freedom, but we must remember that means having to face resistance.

Why Resistance Is a Blessing

As mankind is moving into outer space, scientists are finding something very interesting. When humans are in space for several weeks or months, their bodies begin to weaken. Without gravity to overcome, their muscles get weak.

We find it difficult to get out of bed some mornings; we feel so heavy. Why do we feel heavy? Our physical strength is having a difficult bout with gravity. But if we didn't have gravity, or resistance, we would become so weak that we couldn't move.

Gravity, or resistance, is a blessing in disguise. Resistance and trouble are necessary. And self-discipline is necessary for us to learn to live a selfless life. If we wish to become partners or Co-workers with God, we must learn to accept resistance and learn how to work around it.

Resistance may come from our enemies or from our

friends. It may come between a RESA and a Higher Initiate. But there is a way to make things work. And this way is found in practicing divine love. This year, find ways in which to live divine love.

I asked the board members to speak to you about where we stand. It's something very necessary—funding the Temple now that it's dedicated. We do have to pay our own way; this is important.

27
Giving to ECKANKAR

We have a Temple now. At a recent board meeting, some of the board members talked about initiates coming to them and asking about the cost of building the Temple. "How much do we still owe?" they asked. The board members came to me and said, "We want to recoup this expense."

I asked them to speak to you about where we stand. It's something very necessary—funding the Temple now that it's dedicated. We do have to pay our own way; this is important.

I remember that a long time ago I gave to the Sedona building fund when the Seat of Power was to be there. I gave until it hurt. Pretty soon you ask, "Does this go on forever, or is there a goal?" I've asked the board members to give you our goal and let you know that there is a light at the end of the tunnel.

Vahana Teams

At the Temple dedication I mentioned that I was establishing missionary teams, Vahana Teams. I've asked the RESAs to set up Vahana Teams—of three to nine people—at the regional and local levels. I call them *teams* instead of *councils* because a council denotes a stable spiritual force and a team is active, dynamic. A team is a group oriented toward movement.

I've mentioned the different margs, or areas of spiritual service, before. As time goes on, we're going to find that some people are more inclined to follow the way of the missionary. Others like to be the teachers of ECK. Others prefer the Bhakti Marg. They might work with people who are less fortunate in some way; they might give love to those in hospitals. There are others who like to serve ECK through their writings—plays, articles in a newsletter, and writing articles and novels for the public. That is one aspect of the Giani Marg.

Not everyone has the talents or interest to work in the Giani Marg. Or the Arahata area. I think you'll find you concentrate in a certain area, though you also have interests in other areas. As time goes on this can change, and you may work in different areas of ECK service. This is part of the development of a spiritual path.

What We Offer the Seeker

Vahana Teams in ECK work under the direction of the RESA. There is a team leader and as many members on the team as are needed. In larger areas, there will be more people, maybe nine members, on the team. Areas with fewer ECKists may have only three members on a Vahana Team. We can have a team that's fairly flexible, that's sensitive to the spiritual needs of the community, that will draw on the programs we have developed.

For instance, they might decide to set up a series of talks. They could show one of the ECK videos, such as the dream video. We developed the videos to give a consistent approach to the ECK teachings throughout the world. There's an advantage to that.

But there's also a disadvantage if the videos are the only thing you use for your introductory presentations. The leaders in an area might stop knowing how to relate to the people in the community. People walk in, there's a machine, and soon the only one talking to people about ECK is the machine. If you play the tape for twenty or thirty minutes, then turn off the machine and say, "That's it, folks; you can go home now," that's not quite ECK. The search for truth actually goes from person to person. You can show a video at an introductory meeting, but I think the people who come there would really like to talk with a human being.

People like what they hear from the video if there's a person-to-person presentation first. But if there's only the video, they may say, "Sounds like you're pushing ECKANKAR on me."

We developed these videos with the best of intentions. But as time goes on, we're going to find they work better for some situations and not as well for others. Some chelas have found it works to give a presentation on dreams, then say, "This ends our presentation on dreams. We also have a video available on the dream teachings of ECKANKAR. If you'd like to stay for this, you're welcome." They let people know that now they're going to be talking directly about ECK.

We continue to develop our presentations to the world. But, like you, I still feel that the best link with another seeker of truth is you, yourself. Because you were also a seeker. You know what it was like to come to a teaching and say, "I have spiritual needs. What have you to offer me?"

Four Celebrations of Life

Throughout the history of the human race there have evolved four celebrations of life. One is when Soul comes into the world at birth—this is the first celebration. The second celebration is when a child moves from childhood to adulthood during puberty. It is a rite of passage. The third celebration comes with marriage, when an individual is looking to complement himself or herself and sees this complement in another individual. The fourth celebration is when Soul takes leave of the physical plane during translation. This is a celebration of life because leaving here is the beginning of a new life.

These four celebrations of life are at the heart of the activities of mankind. Under one form or another, this has been the basis for what people do. As they go through life, they naturally enter these stages and there is some kind of rite or celebration to help them. Each stage is a rite of passage, a way of coming into being.

Youth Vahanas

In the future the youth of ECK are going to be our best missionaries. I would ask the RESAs to include at least one youth on each of these Vahana Teams, if possible. I feel the driving force behind the missionary program of ECK will be the young people of ECK.

They helped a lot in putting together the video *Inquire Within.* Then they went out and tested it at the University of Minnesota. The people who came liked it because it was nonthreatening. It was just other youth sharing their views on what they expected from life, what they found in their relationships, and what they liked about ECK. The youth video is going to touch others.

It's important to understand how people think, but I believe it's more important to understand how they act. People will tell you what they think—that they believe this or that—but you can pretty much see how they believe by how they act. You who are going to be on Vahana Teams will need to be very sensitive to how people act. Not what people say they do, but what they actually do. What do they want from a spiritual teaching? What did they want from their own religions but never found?

What Is Burnout?

In the last few years it's been stylish to say, "I'm burned-out." I should point out that burnout comes when people do something out of duty, when the love element recedes into the background.

I recognized that we would be going through a very difficult time when we established the RESA structure. One of the necessities of setting up a worldwide field organization is getting charters. The work becomes legally oriented, and it is very hard. Sometimes people said, "What does this have to do with the mission of ECK?"

You have to set up a good foundation before you can go anywhere. Now that we have the RESA structure, now that we have the Temple of ECK, we have a good foundation upon which to set the missionary effort, the teaching effort, the charitable effort, and the wisdom effort. We have a solid base now. It took a long time to establish it.

Needs of the Heart

While we were setting up all these things, when it was hard going, the good-hearted chelas sometimes worked out of duty to ECK rather than out of love. When it was hard going, you got very little thanks. But now we can go out into the world and find seekers again. We have entered into the Year of the Vahana, the missionary era. Once this element of love comes forward again, we're going to find there is a lot less burnout.

When the missionaries find the seekers, they'll turn them over to the teachers. The teachers will tell them or show them what the principles of life are all about, and how love is actually the basis for life. And when people get a little foundation in the principles of ECK—how to live ECK and act in ECK—then they will be qualified to be part of the wisdom path and the Bhakti Marg, the love path.

The Stories from the Heart videos answer the needs of the heart. They are perhaps not the best, most professionally produced tapes, but there has been a great demand for them. This is because you, in your hearts, have felt that this is what the teachings of ECK are all about. It's about people meeting life, doing the best they can, and learning as they go. It's about becoming better spiritual beings. You train as you go. This is the whole point to being a Co-worker with God.

I think that if you are any kind of writer, you will see the shortcomings in your own writing. You will see what it should be and what you wish it were. And the next time you work on it, you get closer to this ideal. In ECK, too, you strive for perfection.

28

You Are Always Learning

A young woman works as a hostess at a restaurant. She enjoys watching people and the different things they do and say. Many times she's the one who has to deal with them when they're upset. When a waitress has to serve too many tables and a customer doesn't get the service he expected, he complains to the hostess. She has to stand there and be very impartial, no matter what kind of verbal abuse the customers rain on her.

She says that sometimes people will just get upset. They will complain about anything, even the wallpaper. She says it has absolutely nothing to do with the food or the service.

The door that leads out of her restaurant is a little tricky. At times it sticks, then suddenly opens; at other times it does the opposite. She especially likes to watch angry people going out that door. They hit the door going really strong. The door is a little hard to open, so they give it all their strength. Then the door lets go, sending them flying out into the street.

As calmly as ever, she stands there and smiles, "Have a good day."

Recording Stories

A new book is out at this seminar, the *Cloak of Consciousness,* Mahanta Transcripts, Book 5. It is a record of talks I have given at ECK seminars. When I give talks, I try to use images and stories, so that someone listening will be working with strong images of how ECK works in their daily life.

Cloak of Consciousness is full of stories about you, about your lives. My role is mostly that of an ECK chronicler; I put together the chronicles of ECK. These chronicles are of your lives, what you go through, and what you've learned.

Some of the wisdom you come to individually is most profound. I use these stories in my talks because I feel that the richness of ECK is coming out in your lives. It's coming out as you learn things. You have an experience, and by the end of your experience you are somehow different. You have learned something.

Learning about Yourself

John Truby is a teacher of story structure. A number of ECK writers are familiar with his study courses. He said that a very good story is one in which the character is neither good nor bad. The character then goes through an experience or a series of experiences. By the time the character comes to the end of the story, he has learned something about himself that he has not realized before. This is also what is happening each time you have an experience as a chela in ECK.

Usually when I pick a story to tell, it's something out of the ordinary, something that doesn't happen every day. The sharper the experience, the stronger the lesson. Because of the plus element in ECK, even the spiritual leader of ECKANKAR is always learning. I am learning. This means no matter how far you go in the worlds of God, you never get it all. You never reach absolute wisdom. Because of the plus factor, there is always one more step.

Learning about Others

The other new book at this seminar is *Earth to God, Come In Please*... It's a compilation of stories primarily from the *ECKANKAR Journal* over the years. I like the stories in this book because they are your own chronicles of your spiritual life.

The cover is my choice. I looked at it one day and said, "The main body of the cover is two stripes of a light, clear yellow." There was all kinds of reaction, because our book covers are very tasteful. But this one is more dynamic, stronger graphically. The others are beautiful; this is stronger.

My wife said, "These are stories of ECKists from all around the world. It's about people trying to get some connection with God. What if we showed the world between the two yellow stripes?" So we asked an artist to do the illustration, to show how it looks from the higher view. When people around us think of God, it's usually of God up there somewhere looking down. So "Earth to God, come in please..." is earth speaking, and we are looking at it from the view on high.

Earth to God, Come In Please... would be a good book to give to people. It is a collection of phenomenal spiritual insights and experiences. I just don't see phenomenal experiences like that chronicled anywhere else, unless you delve into the straight psychic, and frankly that's sticky. Occult stories were great in the seventies, and there are a lot of people who still like them today. But when you read them, it feels like you got your hand on flypaper.

The consciousness has undergone quite a change since the seventies. When I write I have to catch up, freshen everything for the new age. I'm writing a series of discourses called *Letters of Light & Sound 1,* which are shorter by a third than earlier discourses I wrote, and with bigger type. I'm doing this in deference to our quicker age, where things have to go quicker and be easier to read.

When ECK Taps You on the Shoulder

Things come up to stop my writing, in the same way that you have things slow you down. I put in a lot of time in front of the computer keyboard. I use a notebook computer and am amazed that so much can be loaded on this tiny machine! If we had talked to people about this kind of technology back in the thirties, they simply would not have understood a word we were saying.

It's the same as when we talk to people today about ECK principles. They don't quite understand what we're saying.

So I was sitting in front of my computer putting the finishing touches on one of these new discourses. These discourses are on issues. It's a different approach—whenever there's an issue, there's conflict. The topic this time was the limits of sin. And I was explaining how there were weaknesses to the whole theory on sin.

At that point I just sat back to wait and see what the ECK had for me to do, and It said, "A quote." So I asked, "A quote from what?" "Shariyat," It said. So I picked up book two of *The Shariyat,* turned to the index, and found a quote on sin that fit everything I had said up to that point. But I'm always curious to see what the quote means in context, so I read on to the next paragraph.

In the discourse I'd been writing about how the teachings of sin are out of date. The next paragraph in *The Shariyat* said that the "religious concept of man's iniquity in sin is archaic." This was even more in accord with what I was saying in the discourse. And then there were other parallels to things I'd written in language for today that was in *The Shariyat* in the more lofty terms. This to me was my assurance. Sometimes I need assurance too, because the ECK doesn't pat me on the shoulder a lot. But sometimes when I'm really stretched, the assurance comes through: "Yes, this is of the Light and Sound. This is the message that is to be for the initiate of ECK who's going to be reading this discourse."

Learning about Excellence

I think that if you are any kind of writer, you will see the shortcomings in your own writing. You will see what it should be and what you wish it were. And the next time you work on it, you get closer to this ideal. In ECK, too, you strive for perfection.

Sometimes I wonder about television sports. In Minnesota we have a lot of hockey players. They keep passing that little puck back and forth, the goalie's got everything blocked except a tiny little space, and some player gets it in there. Someone said that the saving grace for sports on television is that we see excellence. So when I wonder why I'm watching TV sports, I remind myself that I'm learning excellence.

The ECK doesn't always come up and tap you on

the shoulder and say, "Job well done." But I can say it, and I do say, "Job well done." I know it's been hard for many of you to come here, but I think you will benefit spiritually because you made the effort.

What is a life of truth? It's being able to accept the love and joy of the Mahanta. That means that you even like to get up in the morning.

29

Fabric of God Consciousness

==Truth must become a living thing for each of you. And the way it does this is by you consciously becoming one with HU in your daily life. Then you become a living, moving spiritual exercise. This is the quickest way I know to start living a life of truth.==

What is a life of truth? It's being able to accept the love and joy of the Mahanta. That means that you even like to get up in the morning.

This morning I wanted to speak about Reverend Shaeffer's bottle of beer. You might say, "*Reverend* and *beer* don't exactly go together." But this is Europe, and beer is part of the culture here. When my ancestors went to America from Europe, they took much of this culture with them.

A Rite of Passage

When I was about six years old, there came an experience that changed me from being a boy to being a young man. At that time of life, you want to be a young man as soon as you can. As soon as you're six, you're practicing to be thirteen or fourteen. And there is some rite of passage to go through. In many orthodox religions this is known as confirmation. As soon as you go through this ordeal, you become a young man.

Back home on the farm we had a rite of passage too. When you became six years old, you were no longer a baby but a boy with your sights set on being a young man: being a tractor driver for threshing. If a boy could drive a tractor, he was well on his way to becoming a man. The farmers always said, "Let our boys drive the tractors. This exposes them to the whole process of bringing in the grain."

Right Way and Wrong Way

The process of bringing in the grain is a lot like the process of going out into the world and telling people about ECK. There's a right way to go about it and a wrong way. There were the bundle pitchers, usually teenagers. They'd pitch the bundles of grain into the wagon with pitchforks. Sometimes they'd throw two or three bundles into the wagon at once, just to show how strong they were. They'd wear themselves out early in the day. Farmers who had been at it a couple of years went at it a little easier, pacing themselves.

As a young boy driving the tractor, I'd notice how the older men were wiser than the teenagers. I also knew that older tractor drivers had an easier time shifting. At my young age I couldn't push the clutch in far enough, so the tractor gears would grind whenever I shifted.

One bundle pitcher was a man I admired named Mr. Hoffmann. He was also our grade-school teacher. To me he was as wise as the ancient Greeks. He was our Socrates, the wisest among men. My dad liked him, so I did too. He could do no wrong in my eyes. He was the teacher of truth, the one who taught us literature and how to add and subtract.

The other kids in my class would compete to run errands for him. We all wanted to be the one to go to his house and collect his lunch. He always sent two of us to get it. Sometimes we'd walk, or when we had our bicycles we'd ride to Mr. Hoffmann's place. Mrs. Hoffmann would make up the lunch for us to take back with us. I found out later that they fought all the time, so he did whatever he could to avoid being home. This is why he used to volunteer to pitch grain in the summer when school was out.

I had mixed feelings about his being on the wagon behind my tractor. Because I couldn't work the clutch very well, the wagon often jerked and dislodged bundles of grain. The farmers would curse at me. I was torn that this teacher of wisdom should see me being cursed by the farmers.

Passing the Blame

Every noon hour the farmers would quit and sit under a shade tree. A keg of beer would be set up. One day old Gust, the white-haired man who lived next door, told the group, "Reverend Shaeffer's coming today." Reverend Shaeffer was my uncle Walter, but we never thought of calling him anything but Reverend Shaeffer.

He used to play baseball in the thirties. He was so good that his seminary team would play against the professionals. The major leagues even offered him a contract. But I admired him more because he said he was going to be a minister and give the message of God instead of pitch baseballs for money. He was a great man in my eyes.

So here were so many great men, men I respected, taking their break around the beer keg. I respected Reverend Shaeffer for having become a man of God.

I respected Mr. Hoffmann for his wisdom. And I respected our neighbor Gust for his kindness and the twinkle in his eye. But he often got into pranks.

One of the pranks people pulled around threshing time was to put water in a bottle of beer. They had the keg, but farmers went through the keg real fast, so they also had bottles of beer in a milk bucket full of cold water. This particular afternoon someone had carefully taken the cap off one of the beer bottles, replaced the beer with cold water, and carefully put the cap back on.

Old Gust got up to get a bottle of beer for the honored guest, Reverend Shaeffer. When he opened it he noticed there wasn't much fizz to it. His attention was elsewhere though, and he politely carried it over to the Reverend. The Reverend took one swallow, spit it out, and said, "Whoa! This is water."

Although people had played this prank for years at threshing time, everyone was embarrassed. Drinking beer was OK, but giving water in a bottle to Reverend Shaeffer—that was unforgivable. Everyone sat around looking like lost Souls, wondering who would have dared to do this to Reverend Shaeffer.

They looked up and down the line of men and boys, looking for someone to pin it on. There I was, innocent as a newborn babe. Gust looked at me and said, "Harold must have done it." I was totally crushed. I respected and loved Gust so much; he had done so many kind things for me. I was crushed that he could possibly have imagined that I would put water in the bottle. Besides that, I had had a bad time with the tractor, and I was already embarrassed that my wise teacher should think poorly of me.

I felt so bad I couldn't eat, so I went out behind the wagons and hid. Some time later my friend Henry came over. He said, "Do you know who put the water in the bottle?" I said, "I didn't do it." He said, "I know you didn't do it. Mr. Hoffmann did it." This was too much. This great teacher of wisdom had just sat there and let a six-year-old boy take the blame for something he had done.

When Your Idols Have Clay Feet

I noticed that day that a lot of my idols had clay feet. In the rain, clay turns to mud. If people have clay feet they're not going to stand very long in the rain. That day I learned more about truth than I had in all my six years. It was one of those big crises of faith for me.

I had a hard time in school with Mr. Hoffmann after that. I kept asking myself, What is truth? Is this great teacher of wisdom so great? Or is he just another human being who happens to teach school very well and also happens to play pranks very well?

And I looked at Reverend Shaeffer and thought, If he is such a great man of God, he should have known that I wouldn't have played that prank on him.

And I looked at old Gust and thought, He should have known there wasn't a black spot in my heart. He should have known. Why did he pick on me, a poor little kid?

That day I learned a lot of things about life. I learned that these men could work together as a team and get the grain in. They all had talents one way or another, but they also had some failings. When it came to looking bad in front of all the others, these men would gladly sacrifice a six-year-old lamb on the altar of their self-esteem.

First Stage of Co-workership

I've found that the first stage to becoming a Co-worker with God is to become a Co-worker with the Mahanta. As you work with each other, you may find that someone who is a very good teacher of ECK also has some points about him that aren't too good. You look at a person and see all the fine points, but you also know the weaknesses.

You too have these strong points or spiritual characteristics. And you have your weaknesses. It is out of such fabric that the Co-workers with the Mahanta are taken. And from this is woven the cloth of the Co-workers with God.

Co-workers with the Mahanta are strong and weak. But it's for their strengths that they come together. And because of their strengths, they can see the strengths in each other and become even stronger vehicles for God.

On this journey to God, look for the good in each other and you will see more of the good in yourself. As you see more of the good in yourself, you will also see more of the good in others. In this way we can truly become strong in spirit, strong in ECK, and strong in love.

The ECK community itself is going to change in time by becoming broader and—I would hope—of a higher, more refined nature. That means your definition, or awareness, of this ECK community will need to change too.

30
The Community of ECK

A new book, *Riding for the ECK Brand,* is available at this seminar. It's put together from the times I've spoken with the High Initiates as a group.

The idea of the book is this: If you're going to be in ECK, be in ECK. Be someone who stands for the principles of ECK. Otherwise, don't go around telling people you're in ECK. Ride for the ECK brand, or just ride off into the sunset.

Forming the ECK Community

I have said that as time goes on, we're going to see the ECK community form. But actually the ECK community has been here right from the very beginning when Paul first brought out the ECK teachings, whenever two people got together to talk about ECK. From the very beginning, there was an ECK community.

This community is an entity that has a life cycle; it grows up the way a child grows up. And it changes as it grows. Sometimes it'll catch a cold and sneeze a lot, or have other problems. Other times, it'll be in the best of health, doing creative things. But there is a progression to this community of ECK that we are all a part of.

What Brand Are You Riding For?

There are some ECKists who are trying to bring out their own brand of what they think the ECK community is. Some of them have been giving workshops based on *The Different Drum—Community-Making and Peace* by M. Scott Peck. When someone in the audience tries to mention ECK, they are quickly shut up. The workshop then becomes one of these emotional things where, basically, the leaders are people who try to control other people. Since nobody has been paying any attention to them, they take a book like this and try to give themselves authority. They say, "This is a best seller; it has a lot of good principles." In these workshops people then begin shouting at each other and using profanity of the worst kind. Initiates and Higher Initiates are doing this. And you have to ask, "Is this ECK?"

I ask you not to bring books from outside of ECK into the Satsang class and try to pass it off as an ECK presentation when there is nothing at all mentioned about ECK.

I don't like to bring this up, because 98 percent of you would never participate in something like this. But when it happens, I have to point it out to the 98 percent of you. I have to tell you not to let the other 2 percent run the show. Don't let them do it, because that is not ECK at all.

What Is Not ECK

When you have people using profanity, cursing in an open ECK meeting, I don't see by any stretch of the imagination how anyone could call it spiritual. No matter what they say—even if they say, "It has good principles"—it's not ECK. It doesn't have love in it. It tears people apart. It breaks up the community. If anyone is pretending to call this spiritual, it's not. They are not of ECK. They are of the Kal.

These things upset me very much, because I am entrusting you to watch at home that the ECK message keeps its purity and its integrity. Things like this don't happen often, but when they do, I have to let the rest of you know. If someone in your community approaches you with such an idea, tell them, "No thank you." Ask them, "Who are you riding for? Are you riding for the ECK brand?"

There's also been some profanity outside of these workshops. Higher Initiates have been using profanity with other initiates, then trying to pass it off as if it's the Master trying to jar the other initiates and give them some kind of a spiritual lesson. But it doesn't work that way.

If you have to use profanity, go home and do it in your closet. Don't do it when pets or other family members are around. Profanity is an expression of a person in anger. Keep that to yourself.

It's like exposing yourself in public. If you wouldn't do one, don't do the other. If one embarrasses you, then the other should too. If it doesn't, it means there's a big gap between your inner and your outer life. What you're pretending to be outwardly is not at all what you are inwardly, and what you are inwardly is nothing to talk about. In ECK, you're not a real leader. You may have a leadership position, but you are not a leader.

I have to mention this to the 98 percent of you who do not have a problem with this sort of behavior. If you hear one of the 2 percent abusing others or using this kind of language, bring it to that person's attention. Do it in a kind and loving way, but be firm about it.

Coping with Change

Someone sent me a card the other day. They wrote, "I've just about gotten used to 'Amazing HU.'" I wrote a letter back to this person. I said that I had brought out "Amazing HU" to show that a culture—even the culture of ECK—does not rise in a vacuum. No culture ever does; no culture ever did.

In Europe, there was a whole culture that existed before the individual countries that we know of today came about. Then countries formed, and the countries changed borders throughout the centuries. There is almost a continental culture and a culture for each country. But the most important culture is the individual's culture—your culture, who you are.

The Umbrella of Your Culture

You grow up under the umbrella of your country's culture, but it's just one of the umbrellas surrounding you. The biggest umbrella might be the culture of your continent. Whether you grew up Christian or Buddhist, this culture is in your blood, flesh, and bones, whether you know it or not.

When the teachings of ECK come out—whether people like it, believe it, or don't—you have to build on what's gone before. Some people like to think they've made a complete break with the past. They believe that anyone who doesn't make a complete break with the past—and accept the ECK teachings word for word without any regard to what has come before—well, those people must not be in ECK.

You have to understand: Things build. Even though you're in ECK today, if you grew up a Christian, the philosophy of this culture is shaped by people who think in a certain way, by the philosophers. You've been exposed to that in school. You've been exposed to the painters, to the Rembrandts. You've been exposed to the great writers. Even atheists who are in a Christian culture have this umbrella of Christianity over them.

But there's a greater umbrella than Christianity. And this umbrella, of course, is the ECK. That's where the main culture comes from, from the ECK. It shows up as a continental culture, a religious culture, a national culture, then finally in your personal culture. All the cultures are of ECK, but they show up in different ways. One culture colors the next. So you are a complex human being made up of many different currents and force fields, or fields of energy.

One of a Kind

This is why we say that each Soul is unique. You are one of a kind. There is no one quite like you. There are some that are like you in a number of ways, but there is no one exactly like you. That is true of every person you meet too. Each is one of a kind. Once you are formed, the spiritual mold is basically thrown away.

This creation that you are keeps changing every day. Parts are added to you, and parts are subtracted from you. This is the culture. And the ECK community forms from this culture. This culture is an umbrella for the ECK community.

Realize that when we're speaking about the ECK community, it's not something you go out into the world and try to create. It's something that already is. And it depends upon the individual experience and awareness of each member of that community. This means each one of you—all the ECKists in the world. This is the ECK community. It's here—all you need to do is become aware of it.

The ECK community itself is going to change in time by becoming broader and—I would hope—of a higher, more refined nature. That means your definition, or awareness, of this ECK community will need to change too.

How to Be There for Others

A non-ECKist was going through very hard times. Her daughter had been on drugs for a number of years and finally died from an overdose. This person has had contact with ECKists. So when she lost her daughter, she called a Higher Initiate simply to cry. Sometimes that's what you have to do—call somebody up and just have them listen to you.

The mother was trying to contact this H.I. because she wanted someone in ECK to talk to, even though she wasn't an ECKist. The H.I. never returned her call. The mother now feels, of course, that she has never met a group of people so heartless and unfeeling. I know this isn't true because 98 percent of you are compassionate human beings.

But this is part of the ECK community: When someone needs help, you're there. If someone calls you and asks to talk, then just listen to them. This is more important than anything. If someone has suffered a loss like this and is hurting, often they are in shock. They don't quite know how to deal with everything; so much comes up. Do what you can.

Sometimes you can do practical things, like cut the lawn or do yard work. Ask if they need transportation. If you know how to make arrangements to help the family through the crisis, ask if you can help make these arrangements. Do the necessary down-to-earth things, the day-to-day things. And if these people need to talk about their sorrows, just listen.

It doesn't mean that you go into a great lesson on karma. I know they don't need that. They'll either learn from what happened or they won't. It doesn't matter. They didn't ask you for a sermon; they asked you for an ear. So give them an ear and just listen.

Areas of Service for High Initiates

More changes are coming in five to ten years. We will have an active clergy, as we have now. These High Initiates will serve in an active outer role: as RESAs, ESAs, Initiators, and those performing sacerdotal functions like weddings and consecration ceremonies.

Then I'll put more emphasis again upon the Mahdis area as being the spiritual area for those who do not want to serve in the public functions of leadership, because some H.I.'s don't want to. Just because you become a Higher Initiate, I don't want to force you into becoming a member of the ECK clergy, the active clergy, and having to get papers and all that. In the future there are going to be many people who don't want to do that sort of thing, because it doesn't fit them. But there will be others who will want to serve in this capacity and will be very good at it.

I want to make it so you can serve in a capacity that you feel comfortable with. I just want to let you know, so when it comes you don't go into shock. Every time we make a change on this path of change, people go into shock. And sometimes some of them do some shocking things. Considering it's such a path of change, I sometimes wonder. None of us really like change, we really don't. But that is life.

Words and Actions

I appreciate what 98 percent of you are doing. But I do have to point out what the 2 percent are trying to do. There are more of you who are good of heart than who are not. Look for others in the true ECK community and stand up to those who are trying to undermine and infiltrate ECKANKAR. That's the only way to say it. This is the brotherhood of ECK. Look for others who feel the way you do when you say, "We are here to bring unity and harmony, not disruption or division."

People may say they are doing something noble or good, but watch what they actually do and how it turns out. If you see a meeting that has people shouting at each other, that's the proof of the pudding. That's not ECK. Talk to the ECK leaders about it. Try to come to an understanding. As a last resort—if you can't get any satisfaction—write to Spiritual Services at the ECK Office.

I appreciate all that you are doing for ECK. Realize that at the same time you are also growing spiritually. If you weren't, it wouldn't be worth the effort and the sacrifice. But from it, if you can get the love of God—if you can get more love for yourself and others—then it is worth all the trouble.

People want to know more about the Light and Sound of God. Talk to them. Tell them what you can. Help them take the next step.

31
Riding for the ECK Brand

I just met with the youth and the ECK Spiritual Council. They represent both ends of the spectrum in ECK. The youth are just starting out in ECK; the Eighth Initiates have seen the teachings of ECK right from the beginning of this present cycle of ECKANKAR.

Gifts of Energy

This year the fourteen-to-seventeen-year-olds had a dance, and so did the youth eighteen and older. One of the eighteen-year-olds said later, "You know, our dance was really flat. We didn't realize how much we depended upon the energy of the fourteen-to-seventeen-year-olds."

This happens at the next level up, too. The eighteen-to-twenty-five age-group gives vitality to the generation above them. Each generation seems to carry energy, even though it's often unaware of the energy it carries. I think we can benefit from recognizing this cross section of energy within our group and take advantage of it.

Living on the Edge

The youth asked me, "What can we do for ECK?"

I told them that if they really wanted to live on the edge—do something really exciting—they could team up with someone who's been in ECK a few years to give an ECK intro presentation. "You might get stage fright," I said. "You might be so scared that your knees are shaking and you won't even trust yourself to walk to the front of the room to give a presentation on ECK."

"But," I said, "when you get out there, suddenly something comes over you. It's the ECK. It'll put the right words in your mouth." I also reminded them not to walk up there without any plan, depending on the ECK to put words in their mouths. If they're not prepared, It may not. It may have a lesson for them about preparation.

Cultivating Out the Weeds in ECK

This morning I was preparing my notes to speak to the Higher Initiates. Some things are fun to talk about. Other things aren't. Sometimes I get tired of talking about unhappy things. I say, "Spring is renewal. I should feel good. I shouldn't always have to point out these things." But I did point out some things to the Higher Initiates to help me identify those people who don't understand what ECK is about and are pretending they do while they are taking people off the path to God.

At home on the farm, to me the idea of cultivating the corn was always just to get the weeds down. But there was something else, too. After several weeks without rain, the ground would crack. Then the soil would lose its deeper moisture through these cracks.

Cultivators are basically little plows behind a tractor. They pull out or cover up the weeds. The tolerance is set very tight; these little plows run right next to the cornstalks. You try to drive fast enough to do the job, yet not take out too much corn.

So the cultivator covers weeds and also covers cracks in the ground. And it keeps the moisture in the soil so it remains fertile.

Every so often—even in ECK—we've got to put the cultivator on the tractor and go through the field. Why? Because that's how you get good corn. We have to get rid of the weeds. Anyone who is in gardening or farming knows that. It's a law of nature. These are things that you have to do if you're going to take the trouble to till a field and put in seeds. You're also going to have to cultivate it.

This is what we will be doing in ECK too with those people who simply do not know what ECK is all about, yet who are going out of their way to lead other people off the path of ECK. If they aren't going to ride for the ECK brand, they should find a brand they can ride for. They should go find a religion that they feel comfortable with.

A Mouse Nest

A while ago, I took my car in for repairs. The mechanic was replacing the air filter, and he found a mouse nest inside.

The mechanic told me that it isn't uncommon to have a mouse nest somewhere inside the car in cold weather, especially in northern climates. The car comes into the garage, nice and warm; the mouse finds the car, crawls in, and stays warm all night. Then he gets out in the morning.

Apparently this mouse had been living there for a long time. The nest was filled with empty sunflower seeds. Mice don't have suitcases or carts to haul four or five ounces of sunflower seeds at a time. They carry the seeds in one at a time. This must have been a very industrious little mouse.

I've always looked at the car as a parallel to ECKANKAR. To have a mouse nest in there really upset me. So I come to a seminar and say, "OK, time to cultivate the weeds. Time to clean out the mouse nests, because they simply don't belong inside ECKANKAR."

The ECK talks to me, too. It talks in one way or another. Then I go about correcting the never-ending problems that come up because—basically—this is earth.

Problems Prevent Boredom

I don't think you've had too many days without problems in your life. If you did, you'd find yourself very bored. If you find yourself having a day without problems, it's probably the second day of vacation.

When you start a vacation, you say, "Finally, peace." Then it gets boring. After the second or third day, you might say, "It'd be nice to get back to work now. But I really don't want to get back to work yet. Maybe the yard needs a little work. I guess I'll just work on the yard." Actually, you want to get back to work because it's got problems. It gives you a chance to solve a problem that means something.

Some of our hosts at the ECK Worship Services at the Temple never get to see or hear the service. They're stationed out in the lobby or somewhere else; that's their job. Somebody suggested that we should rotate the hosts so the ones who are on the outskirts get to be inside, maybe even sit down and hear the service. But after one service, the hosts asked to go back to work. They said, "That was nice, but we'd rather work."

Why We Must Take Risks

This is the point I'm trying to make. Sometimes ECKANKAR becomes a lifeless path for people because they don't put themselves into it. They don't take risks.

One of the most enjoyable ways that I used to scare the daylights out of myself was to give an intro presentation. They just terrified me. Even when I planned beforehand, I gave some very bad intro presentations at first. Later, I gave better ones.

One time a person came to an ECK intro presentation with his own agenda. He started to argue with me. He wouldn't let anyone who wanted to know about ECK speak. I'm afraid I was not as graceful at such times as I might have been. I got protective of the group, of the people who'd come there to hear about ECK. First, I tried nice words. They didn't work. When he started interrupting other people, I really got upset. I finally just shut down the intro and went home.

It was one of the more exciting intros I gave. After that, I was more scared than ever to give another ECK intro presentation. But I couldn't help giving them because I told myself, "Maybe something interesting will happen this time."

It always did. But each time I learned how to deal with things better; I learned how to deal with people better. I learned to ask someone else to be there with me, for instance. This way, if I didn't have the social grace to do something well, maybe the other person would. Between us, we were always able to work it out.

Where ECK Meets the World

When the youth asked me what could they do for ECK, I said, "If you want to do something really exciting, give an intro presentation. It'll put you right on the cutting edge. You'll be on the edge between ECKANKAR and the world. Out there is where two worlds collide: the ECK world and the other world."

But out on the other side of the screen are real seekers, people who want to know more about the Light and Sound of God. Talk to them. Tell them what you can. Help them take the next step in ECK.

If you're a Higher Initiate or a Fourth Initiate, remember to let the Second and Third Initiates help give ECK intros. Let the youth help too. Work in teams with newer ECKists.

ECK Teamwork

If the youth have never given a presentation before, they're probably going to be nervous. But it's OK to be nervous. Someone who is too confident will probably create a fiasco in another direction—by talking about things that don't relate in any particular way to ECK, this earth, or the universe.

For times like this, work out a cue beforehand. Maybe the senior member of ECK can help out by saying, "OK, why don't I take it for a minute?" If the other person doesn't know how to sit down gracefully, use a stronger cue: Maybe put your arm around the person and say, "Thank you very much for explaining this part. I will take the next one." If that doesn't work, don't work with that person again. You want excitement but you don't want too much. We all get older, and our bodies simply can't take the load they used to.

Fourths, Fifths, Sixths, Sevenths, and Eighths who do ECK intros will find themselves on the cutting edge, on the razor's edge. They'll find the life of ECK, where the excitement is.

Sometimes nobody comes to your intro presentation. Then you wonder, "OK, why didn't anybody come?" But maybe one person comes at the last minute. The person who is cleaning the building may come by and ask, "Are you done here? I was going to clean the room if you're done with your meeting." You say, "Come on in. We're done." And you go away without realizing that the person who came to clean the room was the one who wanted to hear about ECK, perhaps. The ECK brings the right people.

Take a Chance in ECK

If you're ever in doubt about the miracles in ECK, put yourself on the cutting edge like this. You'll see some wonderful things. You'll see the hand of the Mahanta. You'll know the meaning of the phrase "I am always with you."

Take a chance. I mentioned this some time ago. Take a chance on life.

Those of you who feel that giving an ECK intro is the way you want to serve, occasionally work with one of the ECK youth on this. They're learning. Feel the energy they have. Sometimes it can be undirected or misdirected energy because you need to spend so much time on earth before you get a feeling for what is right behavior in a certain setting and what is not.

This ability to recognize what is right behavior does not, incidentally, depend upon age. Just because you've been in ECK nineteen years and the youth you're working with has only been in ECK two or three, it doesn't mean anything. The youth could know a lot more about ECK than you.

The Importance of Listening

If I were to put the Mahdis consciousness in a word, it would be simply *listening*. Of course, when you're giving an ECK intro, you can't listen when it's your turn to talk. But you can listen when the other person's talking. You can listen when people in the audience ask questions. Listen carefully. See if you understand the questions, and then try to answer them directly. Sometimes you can illustrate the answers with experiences from your life—they'll just pop into your mind. You'll find that the Mahanta works with you. But prepare. Prepare something.

Others of you are more comfortable working as hospice workers. That takes a great deal of courage, especially now that the AIDS epidemic is moving along. There's a real spiritual need among people with AIDS. Why? Because suddenly they find themselves with the virus which leads to AIDS, and then how do they spend the rest of their life? They are facing a ticking clock. We all face a ticking clock, but if you're HIV positive, the clock is ticking louder than before. And what do you do with your life? What does life mean?

You ask things like, What is love? What is important?

A Love for All Life

An elderly minister in northern Minnesota gave a sermon on accepting gays and lesbians into his congregation. When he was growing up, this issue was not talked about. People didn't deal with it. People made fun of gays and lesbians. Most would never dare announce themselves in public. And no one ever thought that they had spiritual needs because everyone thought they were damned—that homosexuality was a perversion of the spiritual nature.

But I've seen the behavior of people who were supposed men and women of God, who gave their whole life to God doing some of the most horrible crimes against humanity in the name of the church.

Then we have people—in this particular instance gays and lesbians—who love. They may not love across polarity lines, but so what? What are we going to do next? Be against people who love their pets?

People are funny. We have all these notions about what is right and what is wrong about love. I think if anybody can love, just has the ability to love, we should accept this as an expression of the divinity of God working through the human form.

One time in a talk several years ago I said that gays and lesbians would outgrow that. What I didn't say, because it was less popular, was that Soul will have heterosexuals outgrow that.

When we are in the full consciousness of Soul, these positive and negative elements fall by the wayside. They stay in the lower worlds. These things fall by the wayside for everyone. But in the meantime, we're here, and they're part of our being.

Why do some feel that the heterosexual life is OK and others feel that the bisexual or homosexual life is OK? Maybe there are strong influences of the past. Maybe a past life has come in so strongly that a man feels he's a woman. This person might go through a sex-change operation. Others don't want to go through such an operation: They just want the freedom to be who they are. Why should they pay for an operation? Why can't they have the freedom to exist with other people?

When the minister in the northern Minnesota church talked about this, he knew that he was going to walk head-on into social opinion in his congregation. He looked the issue over for a long time. Finally he came to an understanding within himself where he had to say that people who love God will love God, and they won't judge other people on things that are unimportant.

If the gay life-style isn't yours and someone approaches you, say, "It's not my way." That's all. And if you're gay and someone with a heterosexual life-style approaches you, say, "Let me be. I'm OK." Because if you really love another person, you will let that person be.

I'm not talking about situations where people force themselves upon others. That's wrong, whether it's done in a heterosexual or homosexual relationship. That's power, not love.

Overcoming Prejudices

In ECK, we are unlike many of the other religions. We are a unique spiritual path. Why? Because we have come from every religion. Although there are some converts in every religion, a Lutheran most likely grew up in the Lutheran church.

ECKists come from every religion on earth. Because of this, in ECK we'll probably have people who have prejudices that range more widely than any other group on earth. It's going to take a bigger consciousness to work with each other and let others be.

These prejudices are from our childhood training. They're conditioned; they're burnt in. It's going to take awhile before that karma burns out. That's just the way it is.

Be patient with yourself; love yourself first. Then love others more. Because if you can do that, you can also love God. And if you can't do that, you don't have a chance to find Self-Realization or God-Realization.

I'm speaking here about divine love. I'm speaking about the love that surpasses all understanding. You can't understand it. You just love. That's all you do. You let people be.

Are You an Open Doorway or a Locked Gate?

If you want to take the message of ECK to the world, you have to understand that all kinds of people will come to ECK intros. They're going to be there because they are looking for the love of God.

Depending upon how you act and how you speak, they're going to find the way of truth or they won't. Because when you go out as an emissary for ECK and become a missionary for ECK, you become a doorway. You either become a doorway, or a locked gate. People can either come in, or by your mannerisms you'll keep them out.

How do you prevent this? Do the Spiritual Exercises of ECK as you prepare for your ECK intro presentations. And right before you give the presentation, you may want to do a short HU Chant with the person you're working with. It makes a world of difference, believe me.

The woman on the radio said, "If you keep on doing what you're doing, you'll keep on getting what you're getting. So take a good look at what you're doing."

32
Love Is All There Is

The title for this talk sounds familiar to me, as if I've given it before. Maybe it's because that's the nature of love. You hear it, you feel it, and you say it's kind of familiar—especially after lifetimes without it. That's what we have to offer in ECK: The opportunity to find divine love and bring it into our lives.

Take a Good Look

I was listening to a business radio network. One of the people on the program was a business consultant of some kind. She's run into many people in her line of work who are always looking at other people as being responsible for what happens to them, good or bad. And she says to them, "If you keep on doing what you're doing, you'll keep on getting what you're getting. So take a good look at what you're doing."

It was very wise. It's the same message that I've been trying to tell you: We've got to take responsibility for what we are doing. If a problem keeps occurring in our lives—even if it looks slightly different—it's basically the same old problem. If we would just shave some of the fat off our most recent problem with our work, our spouse, or a child, we'd probably find it's the same old problem within ourselves that has shown up in the past. It usually leads right back to us, even though we say, "Who, me? I'm not responsible."

Developing Our Community

Sometimes we forget that the ECK community is not something we are creating from scratch. It existed from the moment the first two ECK chelas got together and spoke about the ECK teachings. The ECK community is an entity like a human being. It goes through all the normal stages of birth and development, the immature stage of the teenager, and into middle age.

Just like a human being, it changes all the time. It progresses. There are times of strength and times of illness; it recovers and then it has perhaps more strength, more wisdom.

Since the ECK community is already here, all that remains for you to do is recognize that it exists and how it exists. Ask yourself, What is the ECK community?

Are You Being Served?

There's a show on public television called *Are You Being Served?* It's about a community in a department store. I'm in charge of household entertainment, so my duty is to record our dinnertime shows. During that half hour we just eat and enjoy ourselves, and we become part of this community at Grace Brothers department store in England.

It's not a very big community, maybe twelve people altogether. The owner of the company is a very old gentleman in the frailest of health. He serves in the role of deus ex machina, which means the savior who comes in and administers justice of some kind, usually the kind that nobody expects.

The employee at the bottom of the sales staff in the men's department is Mr. Lucas. All he cares about is womanizing. Next is Mr. Humphries; he's gay and one of the most delightful characters on the show. Head of the department is elderly Mr. Grainger, a very lovable but grouchy little bear of a man.

The women's department is run by Mrs. Slocombe, who acts very dignified. Under her is the pretty Miss Brahms. Captain Peacock is the floorwalker. Mr. Rumbold is in charge of the entire floor. The show's writers chose very apt names for these people—traits that are part of the human consciousness. Mr. Lucas stands for lewd cuss. Mr. Grainger is like an old farmer who happened to end up in fashion. Captain Peacock struts around like a peacock. Mr. Rumbold occasionally opens his desk drawer to get some rum.

They're a real community. People with failings, facing problems at work or in the family; sometimes the men are against the women or the old are against the young. Sometimes it's management against labor. Labor is the cleaning man who has all the cash. He knows how to solve things from a very gut level, but there's always a price.

I like the title of the show—*Are You Being Served?* As leaders in ECK and as ECKists, you know the whole point of the path is co-workership, which means to serve. If you look beyond the bawdiness of the show *Are You Being Served?* you'll see what it means to be a part of even the ECK community.

Resolving Your Differences with Others

Sometimes the people disagree with each other, but each person retains his personal dignity. This is important. Allow others to have their dignity, because you would like to keep your dignity as a human being. There are times you aren't going to see things the way others do, but by the end of the show you ought to have resolved your differences and be able to get ready for the next show. This is how life is.

When you get together in a community, you're not always going to see things alike. You aren't expected to. You're unique. But as an ECKist you will want to do what you can within yourself to prevent problems from occurring in the community. I'm talking about changes within yourself, not change out here.

By the end of the show, all the characters are returned to the same places they were in when the show began. Yet there are changes inside the characters; they have grown. This community is present in any sitcom or soap opera or running show. If you need to know what a good community is, watch your favorite TV show.

Watch how the ECK develops community on a TV show, then go to the ECK Center and see how you're dealing with other people. What kind of a member of the ECK community are you? Learn from the TV show, from the people you like there and the people you don't like. Ask yourself, Am I the lovable character or am I the unlovable character? Am I sometimes lovable and sometimes unlovable? You can learn a lot. Just look around you in the things that you like to do in your everyday life.

The ECK Temple in History

An ECK chela wrote an article about the ECK Temple and its historical significance. He captured it very nicely. He's writing like a historian looking back a hundred years, putting the Temple and the community of ECK into perspective from the future.

The Temple of ECK book is going to be like a family album. You're going to show it to your children and your grandchildren. You'll say, "I was there in the beginning. I was there when the Temple was new." Things will change as the years go by; we'll probably add buildings. But these are very special times, not just for a building going up on a piece of land, but for the spiritual significance. I've tried to mention some of it in *The Temple of ECK* book.

Being with Others in ECK

Being part of the ECK community also means being open to other people in ECK. An initiate in Canada had a strong nudge to go to the ECK Center. She kept saying to herself, I don't have any reason to go to the ECK Center. But the urge kept at her. So she finally went.

There was another ECKist at the center who had recently been working off some personal karma with someone else. So this initiate talked with that other ECKist about how this karma had resolved itself. As they spoke another person came into the ECK Center. She was a new initiate. She went over to the books and began quietly looking through them. Then she turned to the other two ECK chelas and said, "I've been in ECK a year, but I don't have any friends in ECK. Where do people go after Satsang class?"

This was kind of a sad commentary. She was asking, "Where's the ECK community?" Life is faster today, and in many cases husband and wife both work, leaving little time for people to get together. The initiate who had had the strong nudge to go to the ECK Center realized that the Mahanta had brought her there to get together with the other two chelas. She would have them over for tea just so they could be together. So they could have a chance to talk and just find out how life is going for them.

When times are tough or when times are easy, it's important to just get together and listen to each other. To be with each other. This is the ECK community too. Sometimes only three people.

When You Hear the Sound

A woman traveled to the ECK Temple and was very excited about attending an ECK Worship Service. But sitting in the sanctuary, she couldn't contemplate. There were too many people around. After the service she decided to take a tour of the Temple. When they got to the chapel, the tour guide said to the group, "You look so comfortable. If you like, we'll just stay here a while and contemplate."

When they sat down, the woman all of a sudden heard the sound of chanting, the way monks used to chant in monasteries centuries ago. Why would they pipe in music like that? she wondered. She looked around for the speakers, but there weren't any. Suddenly she realized the chanting was coming from within her. She was hearing ECK Masters singing.

Often when people hear a certain sound in a place like that, they're making a connection with their past, with a time when they made great strides in a spiritual way. At a time in the past, in a monastery, this individual was making progress spiritually and gave this love for God that has carried subconsciously into this lifetime. She came to the Temple and in contemplation in the chapel heard this chanting. She first wondered what it was, then realized she was hearing the Sound of ECK. This is one of the ways you may hear It.

Life Always Expands

These are the good times in a way. But for many of you, I know this has been a hard year, exceptionally hard.

Someone backstage said to me, "Happy tenth anniversary." It caught me by surprise because I live moment to moment, and I plan ten years ahead at the same time. Except for occasional remembering, I usually don't spend that much time in the past. I'm fully in this life, trying to figure out what the patterns of life are. Because I too am continually learning.

Life is that way. It's always expanding. There's always more to find, to learn, to do. It doesn't stop. It doesn't stop with me, and it shouldn't stop with you.

This is being the HU. The Sound must always be in your atoms. It must be with you when you're driving, when you're at work, when you're home eating a meal with your family. The HU and you must be one and the same.

33
Be the HU

We've bitten off a big mouthful to take the teachings of Light and Sound to the people of this world. Light and Sound equals divine love, so when we're being channels for Light and Sound, we're actually bringing divine love to people. Sometimes, as we give this love to others, we never mention Light and Sound. But it all goes together.

Serving with Love

We're missionaries in a new sense. We are not preaching something at people that they don't want to hear; we are serving them with love. And this is Soul's purpose.

I hope people don't think they're here to get a better return on their money, so to speak. There's nothing wrong with getting a good rate of interest, but if people think that's the main reason they're here, it's very sad. It's totally selfish.

If you live for ECK and you live for life, life will give you enough to give back to the source of this gift. It'll always come back. There will be enough for you to give to those who need and to those you love.

Truth Is More Than Talk

Talking about truth isn't truth at all. Talking about truth is just talking. Truth is living. But I have to talk about this, and sometimes in your capacities as channels for ECK, you talk about it to others. Because by talking, we can sometimes explain how the ECK works. How does life work? How do the laws of the spiritual worlds operate? Then when people hear your words, they begin trying to use these laws or principles in their own lives.

It's not always easy to make these principles work. The problem is that we so often forget. We forget the simplest aspects of cause and effect. We do something, and life comes back to tell us, "No, no, no!" Or we do something spiritually beneficial, and life tells us, "Yes, do more of that."

When we forget, we slip back into the rut of habit, the way we did things before we came into ECK. Then things get tough. Generally life will nudge you and bump you until you get going in the right direction again. The more stubborn you are, the harder life pushes you. That's when you look around for someone to point the finger at.

Who Is Guiding You?

Life will teach us if we will but listen. We say we listen. We say we listen to the Mahanta, but actually often we only think we listen to the Mahanta. We think we're hearing. Then when things get worse and worse, you have to say, "Wait a minute. Let me reexamine the premise for my life and actions. Am I really being guided by the spiritual principles of ECK, or am I running under the motivation of 'my own inner master'?"

I'm making a distinction here between the Mahanta and what people call "my own inner master." People assume when they say, "my own inner master," they mean the Mahanta. But by the way they act toward themselves and others, it is clear to me that they aren't getting the message from me on the inner. So who is their inner master?

Sharing Knowledge

When I was fourteen I went away to school in Milwaukee, Wisconsin. It was many miles from our farm and the life I had known. I'd never been away from home before. It was quite a shock. For some people, this kind of experience is very enjoyable; for others it isn't.

At school I got a lot of knowledge. I got so smart I could hardly stand myself. I got enough good grades to help my bad grades, so that I could survive and move on to the next year. About my second year, I took a biology course where we learned the anatomical difference between men and women. What wonderful knowledge, I thought.

So on the next trip home to the farm, I tried to figure out who needed this information most of all. Out in the barn helping with chores, I spotted my youngest brother. He was about six or seven at the time. He was up in the hay mow throwing down hay. I thought, I'll go help him, then I'll tell him all this great knowledge about the difference between men and women.

My brother was working with a pitchfork, throwing little tufts of hay down the chute. It's very hard to get the tufts loose from the large pile of hay. When the chute is finally full, you stamp it down. It was very cold up there.

As we worked, I told him my great knowledge about the difference between men and women. This was truth, the highest truth, I thought. Since he was just a little kid in elementary school, I felt he needed to know these things. So I told him everything in very scientific terms.

At the end of my discourse, he turned to me. "I don't want to grow up to be a mailman," he said. I was totally humbled. Here was this great truth I'd been passing on to somebody, and he had absolutely no idea what I was talking about.

We finished throwing the hay, and I decided I wouldn't tell anyone else my great knowledge.

Look behind the Lessons

Sometimes it's the same way with the message of ECK. I try different approaches. I'll give very intricate explanations of the laws of ECK or how divine love works. Then I see people going at each other, fighting like cats and dogs. I think, Did they get that out of the talk I just gave? I go home to my wife and say, "Sometimes I really do get discouraged. When I go into great detail about ECK, then people do this sort of thing. And when I tell simple stories about the truth of ECK, a lot of people do the same thing. I'm finding this a bit tough."

I think this is what you find in your life too. At each initiation that takes you further into ECK, you maybe learn some of the lessons of yesterday. But now life offers you hardships you're not ready for. It's usually going to make you a better spiritual person. I guarantee you that if you look behind whatever problem you're having now, there's a spiritual lesson there.

Some people have by mistake gotten into the social

consciousness. By social consciousness I mean this: Something is wrong with their lives, and they figure it's because of some other person doing something to them. They don't understand that it's because of some spiritual failing inside themselves. They have allowed themselves to fall into this set of circumstances. Anywhere along the line they could have said, "I want to wake up from this nightmare."

Sometimes you might have to talk to somebody very directly, with love and kindness, and say: "Hey, you're not treating me like a human being. You're not treating me like another ECK initiate. I thought this was supposed to be a spiritual path. How come you are acting so unkindly toward me?" A very direct approach like this, spoken with love and kindness, will often prevent trouble from going all the way to your breaking point. But people don't know that.

Your Fear Bumper

Inside each of you, there is built this level of fear. And it always goes ahead of you like a bumper in the night. It will bump something, and if you stop right there and address the problem, the bump will be gentle. But if you keep walking, you might soon stub your toe on a rock or boulder. Worse, if you don't listen and stop when you feel the first warning, you might go right over the cliff where the bumper won't do you any good, because you didn't listen to the first warnings of the ECK.

So what do you learn from it? If you survive the experience, you say, "Next time I won't let myself get into such a predicament." Next time it won't be exactly the same predicament, but it will have many of the same characteristics. If you would, just have the spiritual ability to rise above the problem and ask, How is this problem the same as the last one? On the surface, it might be an entirely different problem, but underneath will be the very same thing each time.

That very same thing is your level of fear, what fear you feel inside yourself. Why didn't you face the problem before it got too big for you? Because you were afraid of losing something. Maybe you were afraid of losing your job. You thought: I need this job; therefore I will put up with anything. Then one day it gets to be too much. You get upset, everyone gets angry, and all of a sudden you leave under very bad circumstances.

Personal Battlegrounds

The same thing can happen in a love relationship. Maybe one person in the marriage is a little less tidy than the other. Sometimes the untidiness may be about actual cleanliness, say of the house. Other times, and more often, it's tidiness with the bank account. One person may be very careful about spending money, and the other is not so careful.

This is where the great play of that relationship takes place. This is the battleground. Why are they fighting? Because each person believes that they're having to give up to this relationship a freedom of how to live that they don't want to give up.

Early on, when two people get together, they will have their little fights. Why? Because they're entering into a relationship. When you enter into a relationship, you get many benefits. But you also have to give up to the relationship many of the things you are used to doing in your own way. You don't give them up for the other person; you give them up for the relationship.

And in entering into a relationship with the ECK, too, you have to give something up. What do you give up? You give up the small things that are holding you back spiritually in life. This is what you've got to give up to the ECK. This is called surrender. What do you surrender to the Mahanta? Not your money, not your profession. Those are easy. What you surrender are your personal habits, your way of doing things, your thoughts, your old values. These are the things you must give up to the Mahanta if you would find truth.

Living Life with Joy

And what is truth? Truth is the ability to live life with joy and happiness.

Truth isn't a set of words. Truth is knowing how to live this life, with its troubles and with its joys, and take them day by day. Truth is to love waking up in the morning to face another day, no matter how hard life becomes. If you can do that, you're living truth.

This is what I mean by *the living truth*. It's not the words I speak, nor the words in any scripture, be it *The Shariyat* or the Bible or any other. It's your ability to be happy, to be truly happy. Not to be happy because you have just cheated someone or imposed your will on someone. That is not true happiness, and it will never, ever make you a satisfied human being. If you live a life for the ECK, for other people, you will find that you are most truly serving yourself.

And how do you do this? Again and again I come back to it: the Spiritual Exercises of ECK. I used to give spiritual exercises in my talks for a number of years, but I haven't lately. But I think it's important that people realize somehow, sometime, that they are a living spiritual exercise.

Be a Spiritual Exercise

Every moment of your life, you must be the HU. This is more than just chanting HU. This is being the HU. The Sound must always be in your atoms. It must be with you when you're driving, when you're at work, when you're home eating a meal with your family. The HU and you must be one and the same. And if you make yourself more and more one with the HU, you will find that life is a more joyful place.

I've used many words to try to show you something. I can't give you truth in words. I can give you ideas; I can give you images. I leave this image with you: Live your life as if you are one with the HU, so that every moment of your life is a spiritual exercise. When you are talking to a stranger, when you are with your loved ones, you are a spiritual exercise. You are living and moving in the body of ECK.

And as an atom in the body of ECK, there is a sound that comes from you. That sound is HU. This sound not only comes from you, but it is you. You must know that this body you have is just a shield, a barrier—a heavy, coarse shield, and a barrier which is trying to stop you from hearing and seeing your true identity as Soul.

Your True Identity

And Soul? What is Soul? Soul is a divine part of God, and you are that. All that remains is for you to recognize yourself. And to recognize yourself as a divine part of God, you must first—and more than anything else—recognize every living thing also as this part of God. We are in this Ocean of Love and Mercy.

If there is nothing else than love in life, there is more than enough for all of us. So take this love that I have for you and give it to others. Give it to the world.

Glossary

Words set in SMALL CAPS are defined elsewhere in the Glossary.

ARAHATA. An experienced and qualified teacher for ECKANKAR classes.

CHELA. A spiritual student.

ECK. The Life Force, the Holy Spirit, or Audible Life Current which sustains all life.

ECKANKAR. Religion of the Light and Sound of God. Also known as the Ancient Science of SOUL TRAVEL. A truly spiritual religion for the individual in modern times, known as the secret path to God via dreams and SOUL TRAVEL. The teachings provide a framework for anyone to explore their own spiritual experiences. Established by Paul Twitchell, the modern-day founder, in 1965.

ECK MASTERS. Spiritual Masters who can assist and protect people in their spiritual studies and travels. The ECK Masters are from a long line of God-Realized SOULS who know the responsibility that goes with spiritual freedom.

HU. The secret name for God. The singing of the word HU, pronounced like the man's name Hugh, is considered a love song to God. It is sung in the ECK Worship Service.

INITIATION. Earned by the ECK member through spiritual unfoldment and service to God. The initiation is a private ceremony in which the individual is linked to the Sound and Light of God.

LIVING ECK MASTER. The title of the spiritual leader of ECKANKAR. His duty is to lead SOULS back to God. The Living ECK Master can assist spiritual students physically as the

Outer Master, in the dream state as the Dream Master, and in the spiritual worlds as the Inner Master. Sri Harold Klemp became the Living ECK Master in 1981.

MAHANTA. A title to describe the highest state of God Consciousness on earth, often embodied in the LIVING ECK MASTER. He is the Living Word.

PLANES. The levels of heaven, such as the Astral, Causal, Mental, Etheric, and Soul planes.

SATSANG. A class in which students of ECK study a monthly lesson from ECKANKAR.

THE SHARIYAT-KI-SUGMAD. The sacred scriptures of ECKANKAR. The scriptures are comprised of twelve volumes in the spiritual worlds. The first two were transcribed from the inner PLANES by Paul Twitchell, modern-day founder of ECKANKAR.

SOUL. The True Self. The inner, most sacred part of each person. Soul exists before birth and lives on after the death of the physical body. As a spark of God, Soul can see, know, and perceive all things. It is the creative center of Its own world.

SOUL TRAVEL. The expansion of consciousness. The ability of Soul to transcend the physical body and travel into the spiritual worlds of God. Soul Travel is taught only by the LIVING ECK MASTER. It helps people unfold spiritually and can provide proof of the existence of God and life after death.

SOUND AND LIGHT OF ECK. The Holy Spirit. The two aspects through which God appears in the lower worlds. People can experience them by looking and listening within themselves and through SOUL TRAVEL.

SPIRITUAL EXERCISES OF ECK. The daily practice of certain techniques to get us in touch with the Light and Sound of God.

SUGMAD. A sacred name for God. SUGMAD is neither masculine nor feminine; IT is the source of all life.

WAH Z. The spiritual name of Sri Harold Klemp. It means the Secret Doctrine. It is his name in the spiritual worlds.

Bibliography

"Be the HU." ECK European Seminar, The Hague, The Netherlands, July 20, 1991
"Clear Vehicles for Divine Spirit." Singapore, Singapore, November 13, 1982
"The Community of ECK." ECK Worldwide Seminar, Minneapolis, Minnesota, October 26, 1991
"The Curtain between Cause and Effect." ECK Springtime Seminar, San Diego, California, March 25, 1989
"The Evolving Shariyat." World Wide of ECK, Houston, Texas, October 24, 1987
"Expressions of Divine Love." ECK European Seminar, The Hague, The Netherlands, July 28, 1990
"Fabric of God Consciousness." ECK European Seminar, The Hague, The Netherlands, July 20, 1991
"Following Your Dream." World Wide of ECK, Atlanta, Georgia, October 26, 1985
"For the ECK Arahata." World Wide of ECK, St. Louis, Missouri, October 18, 1986
"Giving to ECKANKAR." ECK Worldwide Seminar, Orlando, Florida, October 27, 1990
"The Law of Gratitude." ECK European Seminar, The Hague, The Netherlands, July 18, 1987
"A Leap in Consciousness." ECK European Seminar, The Hague, The Netherlands, July 20, 1985
"Love Is All There Is." ECK Worldwide Seminar, Minneapolis, Minnesota, October 26, 1991
"The Mission of Soul." Tauranga Regional Seminar, Tauranga, New Zealand, November 13, 1985
"A New Level of Awareness." ECKANKAR International Youth Conference, New York, New York, April 18, 1987
"Opening the Loving Heart." ECK Springtime Seminar, Anaheim, California, April 2, 1988

"Partners with Life." ECK European Seminar, The Hague, The Netherlands, July 29, 1989

"Path to Self-Mastery." African Seminar, Lomé, Togo, Saturday, August 7, 1982

"The Purpose of Soul Travel." Melbourne Regional Seminar, Melbourne, Australia, November 5, 1983

"Responsibility and Spiritual Freedom." ECKANKAR International Youth Conference, Toronto, Ontario, Canada, April 6, 1985

"Riding for the ECK Brand." ECK Springtime Seminar, Washington, D.C., April 18, 1992

"Riding the Waves of Change." South Pacific Regional Seminar, Sydney, Australia, November 10, 1984

"Service to Something Greater." World Wide of ECK, Washington, D.C., October 27, 1984

"Soul Equals Soul." ECK European Seminar, The Hague, The Netherlands, July 29, 1989

"Spiritual Co-workers." Hawaiian Regional Seminar, Honolulu, Hawaii, November 17, 1984

"Spiritual Healings." ECK European Seminar, The Hague, The Netherlands, July 30, 1988

"Taking Action." Orlando Regional Seminar, Orlando, Florida, September 19, 1982

"A True Missionary for ECK." ECK Worldwide Seminar, Atlanta, Georgia, October 22, 1988

"When the Chela Is Ready." ECK European Seminar, The Hague, The Netherlands, July 21, 1984

"Year of Spiritual Healing." ECKANKAR International Youth Conference, Phoenix, Arizona, March 29, 1986

"You Are Always Learning." ECK Springtime Seminar, Washington, D.C., March 30, 1991

"Your Freedom of Choice." ECK European Seminar, The Hague, The Netherlands, July 19, 1986

"Your Life as Holy Ground." ECK Springtime Seminar, San Francisco, California, April 14, 1990

How to Learn More about ECKANKAR
Religion of the Light and Sound of God

Why are you as important to God as any famous head of state, priest, minister, or saint that ever lived?

- Do you know God's purpose in your life?
- Why does God's Will seem so unpredictable?
- Why do you talk to God, but practice no one religion?

ECKANKAR can show you why special attention from God is neither random nor reserved for the few known saints. But it is for every individual. It is for anyone who opens himself to Divine Spirit, the Light and Sound of God.

People want to know the secrets of life and death. In response to this need Sri Harold Klemp, today's spiritual leader of ECKANKAR, and Paul Twitchell, its modern-day founder, have written a series of monthly discourses that give the Spiritual Exercises of ECK. They can lead Soul in a direct way to God.

Those who wish to study ECKANKAR can receive these special monthly discourses which give clear, simple instructions for the spiritual exercises.

Membership in ECKANKAR Includes

1. Twelve monthly discourses which include information on Soul, the spiritual meaning of dreams, Soul Travel techniques, and ways to establish a personal relationship with Divine Spirit. You may study them alone at home or in a class with others.
2. The *Mystic World,* a quarterly newsletter with a Wisdom Note and articles by the Living ECK Master. In it are also letters and articles from students of ECKANKAR around the world.
3. Special mailings to keep you informed of upcoming ECKANKAR seminars and activities worldwide, new study materials available from ECKANKAR, and more.
4. The opportunity to attend ECK Satsang classes and book discussions with others in your community.
5. Initiation eligibility.
6. Attendance at certain meetings for members of ECKANKAR at ECK seminars.

How to Find Out More

To request membership in ECKANKAR using your credit card (or for a free booklet on membership) call (612) 544-0066, weekdays, between 8 a.m. and 5 p.m., central time. Or write to: ECKANKAR, Att: Information, P.O. Box 27300, Minneapolis, MN 55427 U.S.A.

Introductory Books on ECKANKAR

How to Find God, Mahanta Transcripts, Book 2
Harold Klemp

Learn how to recognize and interpret the guidance each of us is *already receiving* from Divine Spirit in day-to-day events—for inner freedom, love, and guidance from God. The author gives spiritual exercises to uplift physical, emotional, mental, and spiritual health as well as a transforming sound called *HU,* which can be sung for inner upliftment.

The Secret Teachings, Mahanta Transcripts, Book 3
Harold Klemp

If you're interested in the secret, yet practical knowledge of the Vairagi ECK Masters, this book will fascinate and inspire you. Discover how to apply the unique Spiritual Exercises of ECK—dream exercises, visualizations, and Soul Travel methods—to unlock your natural abilities as Soul. Learn how to hear the little-known sounds of God and follow Its Light for practical daily guidance.

ECKANKAR—The Key to Secret Worlds
Paul Twitchell

This introduction to Soul Travel features simple, half-hour spiritual exercises to help you become more aware of yourself as Soul—divine, immortal, and free. You'll learn step-by-step how to unravel the secrets of life from a Soul point of view: your unique destiny or purpose in this life; how to make personal contact with the God Force, Spirit; and the hidden causes at work in your everyday life—all using the ancient art of Soul Travel.

The Tiger's Fang, Paul Twitchell

Paul Twitchell's teacher, Rebazar Tarzs, takes him on a journey through vast worlds of Light and Sound, to sit at the feet of the spiritual Masters. Their conversations bring out the secret of how to draw closer to God—and awaken Soul to Its spiritual destiny. Many have used this book, with its vivid descriptions of heavenly worlds and citizens, to begin their own spiritual adventures.

For fastest service, phone (612) 544-0066 weekdays between 8 a.m. and 5 p.m., central time, to request books using your credit card, or look under **ECKANKAR** in your phone book for an ECKANKAR Center near you. Or write: **ECKANKAR, Att: Information, P.O. Box 27300, Minneapolis, MN 55427 U.S.A.**

There May Be an ECKANKAR Study Group near You

ECKANKAR offers a variety of local and international activities for the spiritual seeker. With hundreds of study groups worldwide, ECKANKAR is near you! Many areas have ECKANKAR Centers where you can browse through the books in a quiet, unpressured environment, talk with others who share an interest in this ancient teaching, and attend beginning discussion classes on how to gain the attributes of Soul: wisdom, power, love, and freedom.

Around the world, ECKANKAR study groups offer special one-day or weekend seminars on the basic teachings of ECKANKAR. Check your phone book under **ECKANKAR**, or call **(612) 544-0066** for membership information and the location of the ECKANKAR Center or study group nearest you. Or write **ECKANKAR, Att: Information, P.O. Box 27300, Minneapolis, MN 55427 U.S.A.**

☐ Please send me information on the nearest ECKANKAR discussion or study group in my area.

☐ Please send me more information about membership in ECKANKAR, which includes a twelve-month spiritual study.

Please type or print clearly   941

Name _____

Street _____ Apt. # _____

City _____ State/Prov. _____

Zip/Postal Code _____ Country _____